Touching Hearts, Changing Lives:

Becoming a Treasured Teacher

by
Jody Capehart
Revised and Updated With
Lori Haynes Niles
1999

Group
Loveland, Colorado

Touching Hearts, Changing Lives: Becoming a Treasured Teacher

Visit our Web site: **www.grouppublishing.com**

Credits
Editor: Michele Buckingham
Creative Development Editor: Jim Kochenburger
Chief Creative Officer: Joani Schultz
Copy Editor: Shirley Michaels
Art Director and Designer: Kari K. Monson
Computer Graphic Artist: Pat Miller
Cover Art Director: Jeff A. Storm
Cover Designer: Rick Dembicki
Illustrator: Kate Flanagan
Production Manager: Peggy Naylor

Library of Congress Cataloging-in-Publication Data
Capehart, Jody.
    Touching hearts, changing lives : becoming a treasured teacher /
by Jody Capehart. -- Rev. and updated with Lori Haynes Niles.
        p. cm.
    Rev. ed. of: Becoming a treasured teacher / Jody Capehart. c1992.
    Includes bibliographical references (p.   ) and index.
    ISBN 0-7644-2125-5
    1. Sunday school teachers. 2. Christian education. I. Niles,
Lori Haynes, 1961- . II. Capehart, Jody. Becoming a treasured
teacher. III. Title. IV. Title: Becoming a treasured teacher.
BV1534.C266 1999
268'.3--dc21   99-31564
                                    CIP

10 9 8 7 6 5 4 3 2 1   08 07 06 05 04 03 02 01 00 99
Printed in the United States of America

Acknowledgments

I want to thank my parents, Chet and Donna Kvanli, who allowed me to "play" teacher for hours on end and always believed that I was a "born teacher."

I want to thank my parents-in-law, Paul and Marjorie Capehart, for the gift of their son and for sharing Dallas Theological Seminary with me.

I want to thank all the children who have been such a joy to teach and for teaching me so much.

I want to thank all the teachers with whom it has been my privilege to teach and serve over the past thirty years.

Last, but certainly not least, I want to thank my dearest treasures: my husband, Paul, and our three children, Damon, Christopher, and Angela.

Dedication

This book is dedicated with much appreciation and affection to Dr. Michael Fisher who brought me into the world of church Christian education. I thank Dr. Fisher and everyone at Grace Bible Church in Dallas for allowing me to serve as the Director of Children's Ministries from 1987 to 1995.

This book is also dedicated to the treasured teachers at Legacy Christian Academy in Frisco, Texas. May you continue to leave a legacy of our Lord's love.

–Jody

To my grandmothers Ella Mae Haynes and Edith Stevens, who prayed that I would "rightly divide the word of truth," and to my husband, Ken, who taught me what that means.

I would also like to thank H.B. London and the wonderful staff and congregation of Pasadena First Church of the Nazarene for giving me a small start in a big church that powerfully shaped my perceptions of ministry to children.

–Lori

Contents

Foreword

This is a hard time to be a child. Every day the media report crimes by and against children. Record numbers of youngsters are neglected, abandoned, and abused. Children hurry into adulthood before they are equipped to meet adult challenges. The suicide rate is rising.

This is also a tough time to be an adult who cares for children. Working parents anguish over placing their children in child care. Schoolteachers and parents blame each other for the problems and failures of the youngsters they both love. Physicians struggle to help infants with inherited drug dependency or fatal illness. What is to be done?

Author Jody Capehart describes one way to make an important difference in the lives of children. A treasured teacher who instructs by lesson and by lifestyle can guide youngsters into a relationship with their Savior. This special kind of teacher must have the skill to teach effectively, the love to accept children just as they are, and the spiritual maturity to lead a child to Jesus. This book will be a helpful guide to those teachers who want to develop and devote these qualities to their own ministries.

Let me urge teachers everywhere, the novices and the veterans alike, to sharpen their skills and reapply themselves to the educational ministry of the church. As childhood continues to erode, so do our opportunities to touch hearts that are still reachable and minds yet teachable. There is an urgent need for teachers who will share God's love with his children.

In the time it has taken you to read this foreword, two infants have been born in poverty. By the time you finish the first chapter, an infant will have died in its first year of life. If you put the book aside without finishing it today, by the time you continue reading tomorrow, a child younger than five will have been murdered, and 100,000 children will have gone to sleep homeless. If today was a school day, over 135,000 students took a gun to class.

Now is the time to gain the skill and knowledge necessary to make the best use of the hours children spend in Sunday school, Bible club, and camp.

Now is the time to learn how to build trusting relationships with youngsters. Now may be the only time we have.

Dr. Robert J. Choun

Dallas Theological Seminary

Introduction

As the turn of the century approaches, the surge of the Information Age leads us in an ever-spiraling whirlwind. We are learning more about learning at a pace that's difficult to keep up with. But one thing we know for sure—God's children deserve the best we can offer them, and the role of a "treasured teacher" has never been more important. The objectives of this book are the same as they were in 1992, but you'll find many updated ideas for getting there.

As I look at my own life, I see that God has carried me through a wide variety of teaching experiences. While sometimes I questioned why it took me so long to get where I was going, I now realize that he used each experience and each child to teach me. I have taught every age and most subjects in public and private schools, secular and Christian schools, and in several states and countries. I have taught the handicapped as well as the gifted. I believe God has brought me to church work and, finally, to training teachers around the country. I believe in what I am sharing with you because I have lived it. My endeavor is to make it practical and easy for you to use.

What a blessing to have been partnered for this revision with Lori Haynes Niles! With a combined total of over forty years' experience in children's ministry and education, both of us are more avid about learning than we've ever been. As you read through the pages of this book, you'll find it difficult to determine who's speaking as we chose to use first person, no matter which of us spoke. Our hearts beat with the same message: Nothing is more important than investing in teaching for lives changed by Christ!

We pray that you will find yourself nourished as you digest the content of these pages and that you will come to use all your heart, mind, soul, and strength to honor God through the service of teaching.

Learning About
Ourselves
and
Our Children

Chapter 1
Transformed Teachers

Treasured teachers take time to know themselves, realizing that their teaching styles are based largely upon their own learning styles.

Nature *forms* us,
Sin *deforms* us,
School *informs* us,
But only Christ *transforms* us.
—Benjamin R. DeJong,
Uncle Ben's Quotebook

"Therefore if any man is in Christ, he is a new creature;
the old things passed away; behold, new things have come"
(2 Corinthians 5:17, New American Standard).

So you are a teacher! Me too. Tell me: How did you get here? Maybe you spent several years in a teacher training program, learning everything you ever wanted to know about teaching kids (and then some). Maybe you were simply given a teacher guide and a handshake and sent to the classroom. Whoever you are, whatever your background, we have something in common: Our goal is to be like the Master Teacher, Jesus. When we fix our eyes on him and seek to model him in our teaching, a transformation begins.

Teaching Like the Master

"As Christians, we believe there could be no better teacher than Jesus. His teaching defines what teaching is all about."
—Michael D. Warden,
Extraordinary Results From Ordinary Teachers

In Matthew, Mark, Luke, and John, we read the words "Jesus taught" 45 times. Jesus is referred to as "teacher" 46 times.[1] Obviously, we can learn a great deal from studying the life and teaching of Christ. What were the traits that characterized him as the Master Teacher?

• Jesus came from God. He was called and empowered by the Holy Spirit. As he said in John 7:16-17, "My teaching is not my own. It comes from him who sent me. If anyone chooses to do God's will, he will find out whether my teaching comes from God or whether I speak on my own."

• Jesus prayed daily, and he prayed specifically for those he taught: "I pray for them. I am not praying for the world, but for those you have given me, for they are yours" (John 17:9).

• Jesus loved having the children come to him. He cared for and valued them. At one point, Scripture tells us, "He called a little child and had him stand among them. And he said: 'I tell you the truth, unless you change and become like little children, you will never enter the kingdom of heaven. Therefore, whoever humbles himself like this child is the greatest in the kingdom of heaven. And whoever welcomes a little child like this in my name welcomes me'" (Matthew 18:2-5).

• Jesus used a variety of teaching methods. He lectured (the Sermon on the Mount, Matthew 5–7), led discussions (Peter's confession of Christ, Luke 9:18-27), asked questions (Jesus' conversation with Peter, John 21:15-19), told stories (the parable of the lost sheep, Matthew 18:12-14), used life situations to illustrate points (the example of the widow's offering, Mark 12:41-44), and met one-on-one with people (Jesus' encounter with Nicodemus, John 3:1-21).

• Jesus was a wise steward of his time. He looked for opportunities to teach, and he wisely used the teachable moments that presented themselves. His teaching was timely as well as timeless, as in his encounter with the woman at the well (John 4:1-26).

• Jesus believed in what he was teaching. He was committed to Scripture and directed his learners by his example. " 'Come, follow me,' Jesus said, 'and I will make you fishers of men' " (Mark 1:17). His life modeled what he taught and added authenticity to his teaching.

Seek to Be Teachable

To be a treasured teacher in the pattern of Jesus, the Master Teacher, you must have a teachable spirit. Training is an important part of the whole teaching process.

The best training comes from modeling. Jesus knew this when he told his disciples, "Follow me." In his excellent book *Master Teacher,* Edward Kuhlman writes: "Unlike the situation in schools, where students may seek out a mentor and not find one, Jesus has sought out those he would teach. For those whom he has called, Jesus Christ is *the* Mentor, the Master Teacher above all others. Principally the mentor wants to influence others: he wants to impact lives entrusted to his care. He seeks to form character, mold manners, and leave firm impressions, just as our Lord did with the disciples. Jesus called the 12 disciples to 'be with him' (Mark 3:14). Then in close proximity, he nurtured and developed their capacities and enlarged their horizons." [2]

Of course, you must seek first to follow the mentoring of Jesus. Then seek out an experienced and exemplary teacher who will be a mentor for you. Look for someone who

- is absolutely committed to Christ;
- loves people and children, in particular;
- is prepared to teach;
- is always ready to learn;
- knows and lives by God's Word;
- is empowered by prayer and the Holy Spirit.

Spend time with that person, in and out of class. Team-teach or help out in your mentor's classroom, and observe what makes him or her effective. Ask questions. Be open to input and correction.

Next, make a commitment to formal training. Each of us has ways in which we learn best. Explore your own learning style in the following pages and find a training method that works for you. Then begin your journey into ongoing skill development. Here are some steps you can take:

1. Read books on teaching. Some good ones include the following:

Education That Is Christian by Lois E. LeBar, Cook Communications, 1995.

Teaching to Change Lives by Dr. Howard Hendricks, Multnomah Publishers, 1996.

Extraordinary Results from Ordinary Teachers by Michael D. Warden, Group Publishing, 1998.

The Christian Educator's Handbook on Children's Ministry by Robert J. Choun Jr., Michael S. Lawson, and Howard G. Hendricks, Baker Book House, 1998.

The Dirt on Learning by Thom and Joani Schultz, Group Publishing, 1999.

Joining Children on the Spiritual Journey by Catherine Stonehouse, Baker Book House, 1998.

2. Attend teacher training sessions given by your church. If your church does not have anything like this, urge your Christian education pastor or Sunday school superintendent to explore the options of video training or hosting outside speakers.

3. Attend Sunday school conventions in your area. These conventions provide a wide variety of seminars at a very low cost. Most conventions bring in nationally recognized experts in the field as well as top local people to train and equip workers in the many different aspects of ministry.

4. If there is a seminary or Bible college in your town, check into courses for lay teachers.

5. Make your personal time in the Word a priority, which will help you sink your own spiritual roots deeper.

6. In your weekly preparation of the lesson, allow time to read the additional sections in your teacher guide. A good teacher guide contains background information and many tried-and-true teaching tips that will help you develop as a teacher.

7. Pray for the Lord to train you as a teacher using his perfect curriculum for *you*. Whenever I have prayed this, God has provided life experiences and special people at key times to supply invaluable impromptu training.

Understand Your Gifts

I believe each of us has been given unique *strengths* and *weaknesses* that make us the people we are. We give our strengths back to God to be used for his honor and glory. We come to God on bended knees with our weaknesses, and as we yield those weaknesses to him, he can be honored in our lives (2 Corinthians 12:9).

In addition, Paul says that *spiritual gifts* are given to every Christian by the Holy Spirit (1 Corinthians 12:7). The purpose of the gift is not to lift up an individual for selfish gain, but to build up the corporate body of Christ. We are to use our spiritual gifts to accomplish the work of the kingdom (1 Corinthians 12:8-9).

For some, God's spiritual gift is the gift of teaching. In *Your Spiritual Gifts*

Can Help Your Church Grow, C. Peter Wagner defines the gift of teaching as "the special ability that God gives to certain members of the body of Christ to communicate information relevant to the health and ministry of the body and its members in such a way that others will learn." [3]

So what's the difference between having a natural talent or developed skill of teaching and having the *gift* of teaching? Both the talent and the gift of teaching have to do with communication of truth. The teacher with the talent of teaching can communicate truth and impart knowledge. But it is the teacher with the spiritual gift of teaching who can take the knowledge one step further and help students grow spiritually with the information— who can truly transform lives for Jesus Christ.

How can you tell if you have the spiritual gift of teaching? Consider these questions:

• Do you enjoy teaching? God intends for us to enjoy serving in his kingdom. If you are teaching joyfully, you probably have the spiritual gift of teaching.

• Do you see fruit in your teaching? Is God blessing your teaching ministry?

• Are others encouraging you in this area, affirming that you are operating in your area of giftedness?

In reflecting on my own life, I see how God has led me to be a teacher. Growing up, I was one of the oldest of seven siblings, which meant I was often baby-sitting. This led me to baby-sit outside the home, too. As a young girl, I loved to help my teachers in school and at church, and I played school for hours on end. My idea of a fun outing was to walk around the outside of the nearby school building, studying each classroom through the windows.

God gave me the desire to teach from an early age. But because I was not yet a Christian, I did not have the gift of teaching. When I made a commitment to Jesus, however, the Holy Spirit bestowed the spiritual gift of teaching on me. Teaching is where my heart is!

Go to the Word and read about the spiritual gifts in Romans 12, 1 Corinthians 12, and Ephesians 4. Then look at your own life. To what activities do you spontaneously gravitate? In what areas is God blessing you? Where do you receive joy and fulfillment? Your answers will help you find your spiritual gift.

If you would like a concrete tool to help you learn more about your spiritual gifts, I recommend the spiritual gifts inventory developed by Dr. C. Gene Wilkes called

"DISCovering Your Spiritual Gifts." For more information or to request copies, contact In His Grace, Inc., 4822 Droddy, Houston, Texas 77091, or call (713) 688–1201.

Understand Your Style

In addition to being unique in our spiritual giftings, each of us is inclined to teach in the way we learn best. Take a look at these descriptions, and see if you recognize your own learning preferences.

You learn best when you can see something. You are drawn to teaching with

- visual aids
- colorful books and workbooks
- writing activities
- bulletin boards and posters
- overhead projectors

You learn best by listening and talking about something. You are drawn to teaching with

- lectures
- question-and-answer opportunities
- tapes
- music
- discussion groups

You learn best when you can touch or do something. You are drawn to teaching with

- models
- puzzles and games
- movement
- role-playing
- centers

These three types of learning preferences reflect the three basic "perceptual strengths" or ways people take in information: visual, auditory, and tactile/kinesthetic. You are inclined to present material to your learners in the same way you prefer to take it in.

Now that you know your perceptual strength, let's find out your teaching style—your teaching *personality,* if you will. Fill out the brief Informal Teaching Style Inventory on page 17 to identify your "teacher type." Your learning style tells you how you prefer to take information in; your teaching style gives you a feel for what you do with information once you've got it.

If you have the highest score in column one, you are most likely a Relater— a Miss Tenderhearted or Mr. Talkative. Each of the words in that column describes an aspect of your personality. You have a tendency to be very focused on individual learners and their stories. You remember what it was like to be a child. You love to talk to your students and to nurture their growth. At the same time, you may become easily distracted from your lesson and struggle with discipline. By becoming aware of these strengths and weaknesses, you can be a master of the "teachable moment," effectively relating your message to the real life experiences of your class.

If you have the highest score in the second column, you are most likely a Researcher—a Mr. Technician or Mrs. Tutor. You love the subject material and are likely to spend considerable time crafting your lesson, drawing from additional resources and finding facts that substantiate whatever you say in class. You want to see your students equipped to defend their faith with authority. On the other hand, you may forget to relate the facts you've documented to daily life, expecting the head knowledge to somehow sink into the hearts of your students. By becoming aware of these strengths and weaknesses, you can become proficient in addressing each learning style represented in your class and begin to really connect with each child effectively.

If you scored highest in the third column, you are most likely an Organizer—a temperate-natured Mrs. Thorough or Mr. Tenacious. You are practical and organized, unlikely to become ruffled. Wanting to carry out every detail you are responsible for, you use each item in your resource kit, following the directions as written. But while your commitment to preparation carries you through almost any crisis, you may miss out on tremendous opportunities by being inflexible. You also may be inclined to have difficulty accepting children who don't fit your mold—who are "wild," "messy," or who interfere with your well-laid plans. You are an administrator's dream, but you may fail to connect with your students, leaving you to wonder what you could possibly

Informal Teaching Style Inventory

Look at the following words. Place a number from 1-4 in each box, 4 indicating a word that is most like you and 1 indicating a word that is least like you. Add your total number of points in each vertical column and record the number under the column.

1	2	3	4
sensitive	factual	thorough	inspirational
relational	love research	literal	outgoing
subjective	rational	methodical	aggressive
personable	black or white	habitual	willing-to-risk
storyteller	objective	detailed	independent
spontaneous	serious	punctual	experiential
empathetic	analytical	hard-working	energetic
emotional	logical	sequential	enthusiastic
sincere	systematic	organized	creative
insightful	critical	practical	busy

have done wrong. By becoming aware of these strengths and weaknesses, you can develop a plan for spontaneity and watch the Holy Spirit step in to strengthen your connection to your students.

If your highest score occurred in the fourth column, you are most likely a Doer—a Mr. Tasker or Miss Tornado. You may be involved in a thousand different activities, and preparing for teaching simply gets overlooked—you really don't like that curriculum guide anyway! Your class is never boring, but rarely "on-task." Your energy level rivals that of your students, and that helps you understand their need for frequent surprises and lots of action. By becoming aware of your strengths and weaknesses, you can become an effective, creative teacher who is focused on the significance of delivering God's message to your students in unique and unconventional ways.

What if two scores are the same? Relaters and Doers often share many characteristics, as do Organizers and Researchers. Sometimes we learn the skills of a complementary style to successfully balance our temperaments with the demands of our lives. Many successful teachers find that they show similar scores in all four categories, demonstrating a flexibility of thinking that helps them to relate to all learning styles.

Remember that this is a quick, informal assessment. All of us, like our students, have layers and layers of preferences and propensities that make us uniquely suited to the position God has called us to fill. I hope you can see the beauty of each teacher type. We are, by design, human snowflakes, each uniquely crafted and called to work together for God's purpose. None of us can connect with *every* learner, but every one of us can connect with *some* learners. God in his sovereignty created a plan to supply each child with a teacher intended especially to reach him or her. That is the awesome wonder of God's design of evangelism and discipleship—and the heart of becoming a treasured teacher.

Understand Your Mission

Our commission as teachers comes directly from the last earthly words of Jesus: " 'All authority in heaven and on earth has been given to me. Therefore go and make disciples of all nations, baptizing them in the name of the Father and of the Son and of the Holy Spirit, and *teaching them to obey everything I have commanded you.* And surely I will be with you always, to the very end of the age'" (Matthew 28:18-20, emphasis mine).

While the knowledge of the world and its workings is multiplying at awe-inspiring speed, our subject matter stays focused. Our job is to relate what Jesus commands in his Word to an increasingly complex world, to *make disciples* in this decade and beyond. That will call for all the internal and external resources we can muster, but we are not to fear because Jesus promises to be with us always.

With that in mind, here are four T's for treasured teaching:

1. Be a *torch* of light. Treasured teachers let their light be seen by others. We must be willing to be used, willing to share the light that we have attained through our own walk with the Lord. As we read in Luke 8:16, "No one lights a lamp and hides it in a jar or puts it under a bed. Instead, he puts it on a stand, so that those who come in can see the light."

2. Be *transparent*. We must be open with our students about who we are and what the Lord is doing in our lives. The willingness to be vulnerable can be one of the most effective teaching tools we have. When we are willing to share our mistakes and weaknesses, children listen to us. Why? Because they relate! When they see us being transparent with needs and mistakes, going to God's Word to discover what it says about these needs, and making life-changing re-sponses to God's direction, we become a living curriculum. The written Word shows itself as the living word. Our transparency can help children see, up close and personally, that "the word of God is living and active. Sharper than any double-edged sword, it penetrates even to dividing soul and spirit, joints and marrow; it judges the thoughts and attitudes of the heart" (Hebrews 4:12).

3. Be a *treasure* hunter. We must tap into and uncover what makes each child blossom. Every teaching experience is a treasure hunt, a search to dis-cover what key will unlock the door to a child's lifelong quest to know God. Search with expectancy. God wants you to experience the thrill of teaching!

4. Be *trustworthy*. Our children depend on us to provide a learning en-vironment that is safe both physically and emotionally. Character counts. We must base the practices of our daily lives on God's principles. Our moral and ethical behavior impacts our effectiveness. Do we keep commitments to our-selves and to others? Some of our most needy students may not even be those in our classroom, but rather those individuals that we see in our day-to-day lives who study us to find out what Christianity is all about. Let us seek to be trustworthy in our personal lives as well as our teaching ministry. Let's be committed to being above reproach, through God's grace.

Inner Direction

As you think about these questions, make a note of related personal experiences or Scriptures that contribute to your understanding.

1. Why do you think Jesus used multiple methods for teaching?

_____

_____

2. What goals do you have for improving yourself as a teacher?

_____

_____

3. What is your understanding of your spiritual gift, and how has your understanding matured?

_____

_____

4. What changes can you envision as a result of understanding your teaching style?

_____

_____

5. What personal teaching standards would you add to the Four T's for treasured teaching?

_____

_____

ENDNOTES

1. R.G. Delnay, *Teach As He Taught: How to Apply Jesus' Teaching Methods* (Chicago, IL: Moody Press, 1987), 19.
2. Edward Kuhlman, *Master Teacher* (Old Tappan, NJ: Fleming H. Revell Co., 1987), 75.
3. C. Peter Wagner, *Your Spiritual Gifts Can Help Your Church Grow* (Ventura, CA: Regal Books, 1997), 112.

Chapter 1
Studying Our Students

Treasured teachers take time to learn how to
reach and teach each individual learner.

A treasured teacher allows for individual differences in the
way students learn, and in so doing makes a significant
difference in the individual lives of the students.

*"Train a child in the way he should go, and when he is old
he will not turn from it"* (Proverbs 22:6).

We adults are good at telling children—and each other—what to do. Modern usage of the word "should" implies an imposition of will from an outside source: "You should exercise more," "You should have known better," "You should be happy about that!" So naturally when we read Proverbs 22:6, our thoughts lean toward imposed guidance, and we begin to analyze all the things we want for a child; we begin with the end in mind. And there is value in that perspective! It helps us define our goals for educating children in a godly manner.

But the word "should" has another implication here. According to the Life Application Bible commentary notes, " 'In the way he should go' is literally, 'according to his [the child's] way'...This verse implies that parents [and teachers] should discern the individuality and special strengths that God has given each one."

In this chapter, I hope to give you some tools for discerning those special strengths and how they relate to each student's learning.

The dictionary tells us that "learning" means "to gain knowledge; to become informed; to seek understanding; to memorize; to find out." [1] The encyclopedia adds that to learn is to "change as a result of experience." [2] Putting this together, our goal as teachers of the Word should be to help our students

• *gain knowledge* of God and his Word,
• *become informed* of what God would have us do,

- *seek understanding* of God's ways and principles,
- *memorize* parts of his Word,
- *find out* how God's Word applies to our lives, and
- *encourage change* as the result of an experience with God.

By understanding our students better, we can reach each one with the message of salvation and teach the Word of God so that it makes a difference in each child's life. That is our eternal focus as well as the practical application of our teaching. The more we understand how to reach each learner, the more effective our teaching becomes.

How We Learn

Research says that after 30 days, students remember 10 percent of what they hear, 15 percent of what they see, 20 percent of what they hear *and* see, 40 percent of what they discuss, 80 percent of what they do, and 90 percent of what they teach to others.[3] The main message from these statistics is that the more children can interact with all of their senses, the more apt they are to retain what has been taught.

Young children are naturally multisensory learners. If we observe babies or toddlers, we see them interact with whatever they are exploring with all of their senses—often simultaneously. They will pick up an item, put it in their mouths, smell, look, and get to really know the thing. Teachers of preschoolers find they are most successful when they give kids the opportunity to explore a learning opportunity with all their senses.

As children mature, however, usually between first and third grades, they develop preferences for the way they take in information (the perceptual strengths we discussed in the previous chapter). Still, involving the senses is one key to reaching a learner of any age. We can utilize any sense—even smell or taste. In most classrooms, teachers present visual or auditory strategies first. But we must be flexible; we must teach in a way that unlocks the "gates" to the minds of differing learners. If the "key" we start with doesn't work, we must try another. The beauty of this is that no particular key indicates a child's level of intelligence or ability; a child is not smarter simply because he or she grasps a concept with the first strategy we use.

I remember a little boy I'll call Johnny. He had a reputation for "not paying attention" and "talking too much." He was also having trouble learning to read. With each passing year, his parents became more frustrated as Johnny's self-esteem crumbled before their eyes. His educational future looked bleak—and he was just seven years old!

When he became my student, I discovered it was true: Johnny did talk a lot, and he could be disruptive. He did have trouble doing the lesson page in his student book.

One day as I stood behind him, I said, "Johnny, follow along with your finger as I read the lesson." I read with a great deal of voice inflection. He followed along, and unlike previous times, he knew the answers to my questions when we were finished. I encouraged him to verbalize what he understood of what I read. He knew it!

This event led us to discover that Johnny learned best when given a chance to *hear* the lesson and then *talk* about it. Johnny was obviously an auditory learner who had been taught with visual strategies. He was also greatly helped any time he could *touch* something—as I encouraged him to do by moving his finger along the page. Johnny was fine. We just hadn't opened the sensory gates that helped him learn best.

This was definitely an eye-opener for me. Until that time, I had expected all the children in my classroom to sit still and listen to me and then do their page in the student activity book. If they didn't, or if I had trouble getting them to do it, I would feel disappointed. When I realized that children learn in different ways (adults do, too!), I prayed for the Lord to stretch me as a teacher and help me modify my teaching style to reach other students like Johnny.

As I let some kids talk more and others do more, and as I brought in things for some of them to touch, the transformation in my classroom surprised even me. Over the years I've watched the talkers grow up to become lawyers and teachers. The touchers have become technicians and mechanics; the doers have turned out to be policemen and doctors. I can clearly see why God designed their learning styles in such a special way.

My great-great Aunt Hattie used to twinkle when she'd say to me, "When God made you, he threw away the pattern!" While she may have been commenting on my particular peculiarities, that old-time maxim captures a truth we are well advised to remember: God designed all children to be unique expressions of his creativity.

My teaching mission became to find the special learning gates within each child that would unlock their hearts and minds and then to reach and teach each one for Jesus. Since then, I've become aware of many more keys that have helped me reach more and more children.

There are many good books on the market that explain childhood development, learning styles and processes, and intelligence. Each new element of knowledge combines with others to give us a more complete understanding of how to teach the "whole child." I like to look at each piece of information as though it were printed on a transparent overlay. Remember Volume H of the school encyclopedia set? Under "Human Body" there was a single page printed on regular paper and several pages of thin overlays that allowed you to look at how each system fit into the body and how they overlapped. Each system fit into place perfectly with all the others.

In my mind I see the individual child as the page printed on regular paper. Each of the learning considerations is one of the overlay pages. Instead of the overlays fitting precisely over the page, however, they are turned in many different directions, with no two interfacing in quite the same way. Yet they combine to make a perfect picture.

We are indebted to the excellent research done by people in the fields of education and psychology, including Jean Piaget, Marie Carbo, Maria Montessori, Kenneth and Rita Dunn, Bernice McCarthy, David Kolb, Lawrence Kohlberg, Katherine Briggs and Isabel Myers, Anthony Gregorc, Kathleen Butler, Howard Gardner, and James Fowler, among others. Let's try to pull together some of the best principles from each of these researchers, "overlay" the information, and see how it can be applied in a church classroom.

While many of the researchers I've cited are not Christian, the work they've done nevertheless points to God—showing how completely and with what complexity our Creator has formed us.

The Whole Child

Understanding "Age-Appropriate"

It almost goes without saying that children at different ages have different needs. Yet one of the most frequent complaints I hear from older children when I ask them about Sunday school is that it is "babyish." Certainly those same kids wouldn't say that the Christian life itself is babyish! In fact, most of them love to hear about sports heroes and media figures who profess faith in Christ. At the same time, they say that their pastors' sermons are "too hard for kids to understand."

The issue is age-appropriateness. To understand what is age-appropriate, we need to have a basic understanding of the progression of stages in four well-documented areas of development: intellectual, psychosocial (how a child feels about himself and others), moral, and spiritual.

Two researchers who have dramatically impacted our views of child development are Jean Piaget and Erik Erikson. The chart on page 26 summarizes the stages of *intellectual* and *psychosocial development* in childhood proposed by these researchers. The ages are not absolute, but both theories propose that the stages progress in order.

In his book *Raising Good Children,* Thomas Lickona draws on the work of Damon, Selman, and Kohlberg to present four predictable stages of *moral development* during childhood: [6]

• **Stage 0—Egocentric Reasoning**—lasts through the preschool years. Children in this stage are morally motivated solely to get their own way. Their behavior isn't selfish: They simply don't have the ability to think beyond their own needs and desires.

• **Stage 1—Unquestioning Obedience**—begins around kindergarten age. Children in this stage are morally motivated to do what they are told. (This stage is much too short, and some children seem to fly right past it!)

• **Stage 2—What's-in-It-for-Me Fairness**—applies to early elementary students. Their moral reasoning level allows them to work within the framework of "I'll be nice to you if you are nice to me."

• **Stage 3—Interpersonal Conformity**—applies to children in the middle and upper grades. Their moral reasoning focuses on meeting the expectations

Age	Piaget's Stage (intellectual development)	Erikson's Crisis (psychosocial development)
Birth to about 18 months	Sensorimotor or practical intelligence—The infant progresses from reflex responses to trial-and-error learning.	Trust versus mistrust—Infants learn to trust through having their physical needs met and having mutual interactions of initiation and response. Trust is foundational to all other emotional and faith development.
1 to 3 years	Preoperational or intuitive intelligence—Children are egocentric, use intuition rather than logic, learn more through action than through language, and focus on one thing at a time. They can't "think backwards" to analyze cause and effect.	Autonomy versus shame and doubt—Children need a sense of independence and the ability to control aspects of their environment within firm limits for safety and security. They need to learn to balance free choice and self restraint.
3 to 6 years	Preoperational stage extends through age seven or eight.	Initiative versus guilt—Children learn to plan and carry out purposeful activities, begin to establish perceptions of their own individuality, explore how their behavior impacts others, and begin to recognize the "inner voice" of conscience.
6 to 12 years	Concrete operations or concrete intellectual operations—Children develop logical but not abstract thinking, begin to master the concept of time and to recognize the viewpoints of others.	Industry versus inferiority—Children move from being engrossed in play to being interested in work, creating tangible products, and performing skills. They need to hear "good job" and receive recognition.
12 and up	Formal operations or abstract intellectual operations—Children can think about ideas without concrete examples, can think about their own thoughts, and can generate a range of solutions based on possibilities rather than examples.[4]	Identity vs. role confusion Intimacy vs. isolation Generativity vs. stagnation Integrity vs. despair [5]

of people they know.

Three other stages follow these in adolescence and beyond. Lickona proposes that children don't necessarily move vertically from one stage to the next, but instead have jumps across the stages, trying out higher levels of moral reasoning before it becomes their dominant moral stage.

To be treasured teachers, we always must challenge children to move on to the biblical moral reasoning Jesus calls us to. By understanding the predictable moral development patterns of children, we can relate these biblical concepts more effectively. To encourage jumps of morality without taking into account the spiritual power available to us through the Holy Spirit is to set a child up for tremendous guilt.

James Fowler gives us a look at the stages of *faith development* that overlap the other developmental stages we've just reviewed.[7]

• In infancy, **primal faith,** based on confidence in trusting relationships with caretakers, begins to form babies' images of God.

• In early childhood, **intuitive-projective faith** emerges. In this stage, children begin to use language to express their first conscious images of God. They stretch their imaginations to make God fit life as they know it. Their conceptions of God may be magical, yet profound. For example, when I worked with children who were going through therapy for cancer, one little girl who had a brain tumor drew a picture of herself with a big, red cross on her forehead. When I asked her about it, she explained that God had put Jesus' cross on her head to make her well.

• As children begin to develop logical thinking skills, they enter what Fowler calls the **mythic-literal** stage of faith. They begin to attribute to God their own sense of fairness and develop an immature but complex systematic theology based on "If I do this, then God will do that." These elementary-age children usually can't articulate abstract concepts of God, but they can certainly tell you about what God does. It's hard for children in this stage to truly understand abstract concepts, such as grace and mercy, unless they can attach it to a concrete personal experience.

When we keep in mind the basics of development in these four areas, we can challenge children to grow without over- or underestimating their abilities in a way that leads to frustration for us and for them.

I've found it helpful over the years to encourage teachers to put developmental information into perspective by using or adapting what I call "focus attitudes" for Christian education. These are internal feelings we want children to develop, whether they can articulate them or not. These attitudinal goals—stated in the child's words for simplicity—form a filter for what we plan and do with each age level.

Focus Attitudes for Christian Education

	Target attitude: God wants me to have a joyful life.	Target attitude: Church is a place where I want to be.	Target attitude: I belong to God's family.
Preschool	God loves me, and Jesus is my friend.	Church is a safe place for me.	I am loved by God's family.
Early Elementary	God knows best, and Jesus helps me know God.	Church is a happy place for me.	I participate in God's family.
Late Elementary	God has a plan; Jesus helps me to fit into God's plan; the Holy Spirit helps me carry out God's plan.*	Church is a fun and supportive place for me and my friends.	I reach out to others through God's family.

*An understanding of the role of the Holy Spirit often doesn't come until adolescence, because to conceptualize the Holy Spirit requires the ability to think somewhat abstractly.

Notice how these attitudes progress from a child's natural self-absorption through healthy peer interaction. Each attitude builds on the integration of those of the previous stage and forms a firm platform for growth into maturity. I believe that when these attitudes are firmly established in childhood, they will undergird a lifetime relationship with God, drawing a person back to God even in rocky times. Developing these attitudes is like tilling, fertilizing, and preparing good soil that will be receptive to the Sower's seeds (Matthew 13:1-9).

Once we have a handle on the fundamentals of age-appropriateness, which are really very similar for all learners, we are ready to jump into some of the areas in which each child is very different.

Understanding Personality

All of us see life through the grid of our own personality. That grid often colors our perceptions of how things are as well as how we think they should be. Obviously, we can't be characterized as simplistically as the following descriptions suggest, but let's take a look at a few general personality types.

1. Fun Lovers

Fun-loving children measure the validity of a situation by the degree of fun it is. If they had fun, then they must have learned! These learners are generally "people people," and they love interacting with others. If you teach in a very serious manner and allow for little interactive time, these children are probably not having fun. Thus, they may reject what you have taught them simply because it wasn't fun.

Does this mean that you have to prepare a three-ring circus in order to teach Sunday school? No, but it would be wise to do something fun at some point in your hour of teaching!

I remember a teacher I'll call Mr. Huckle. He was very thorough in his preparation and, by many standards, was an excellent teacher. But many children did not enjoy his class. One day one of the students brought in a cartoon book about church life. Why, even Mr. Huckle got a charge out of some of the sketches! He wisely bought his own copy of the book, made up a transparency each week from one of the cartoons, and shared it at the beginning of each class. Such a little thing—but it transformed the children's responses. They began to look forward to his class just to see which cartoon he had picked for them.

2. Perfectionists

Perfectionist learners are the idealists; they can see the way it "should be," and they want to do it right. They are often more serious than fun-loving students. They may even get stuck on an issue, whether major or minor, because of a temporary "paralysis of analysis." They can see how a project should be done, and then they begin to question their own ability to pull if off.

These children don't run up and hug you as the fun-loving ones do. In fact, you can't always tell if they like you. They are often so serious! However, it is usually the parents of a perfectionist who tell me how much their child looks forward to getting a hug from *me*. Often the kids who need our affection and encouragement the most are the ones who show it the least! With a little encouragement, perfectionists can produce great art work, engage in in-depth thinking, and spout amazing pearls of wisdom.

3. Control Seekers

Control-seeking learners generally want control at any cost. You can see it in their eyes! They are often the discipline problems because they want to be in charge and will do anything to win a battle of wills. We need to give them tasks to be in charge of that *we* have defined. The words, "You may be in charge of…" work wonderfully. We just want to be sure that we have something ready for them to be "in charge of" so they won't try to get control of the entire class.

As teachers, we must teach these children how to submit to authority. True leadership comes by learning to follow first. This is a very difficult lesson for control seekers to learn. They truly give us an opportunity to practice our patience.

4. Peacemakers

These learners are wonderfully easygoing. While the fun lover is trying to have "fun," the Perfectionist is trying to be "perfect," and the Control Seeker is trying to get "control," the Peacemaker simply "goes with the flow."

As wonderful as they are to have in class, however, be aware of two potential liabilities with these students. First, they *can* be stubborn if pushed too hard, especially by a controlling teacher. Also, they are often the ones who make little witty jokes behind your back. When you turn around and glare at the Control Seeker or Fun Lover you are *sure* said it, the Peacemaker will look innocent. However, he may well be your culprit! The Peacemaker simply has a delightful sense of humor and loves sharing it.

We are each so vitally needed in the body of Christ. We need those who bring love and joy into the body. We need the deep thinkers and creators. And we need the leaders. When I watch these strong-willed control seekers grow up and see God calling them into leadership, I become even more committed to guiding them to be godly leaders.

Of course, I remember how they exhausted me when I first began to teach. I so wanted to have discipline in my classroom, and these children seemed relentless in their desire to control! When I learned how to challenge them to godly leadership, channeling that abundant energy by giving them something to be "in charge" of, my job became much easier.

Brain Basics

All learning, of course, is tied to the operation of the brain. Today, technology has opened up incredible new ways of exploring the actual work of this amazing organ. Let's look at the most basic categorization of neurological functioning: hemispheric dominance.

Ask yourself: If you have a difficult project to do that requires concentration and some studying, where would you go to do this work? Would you seek out a place that is quiet, contains a desk or table, and includes bright light such as from a window or lamp or both? Or would you go to a place that provides some background sound, contains your comfortable chair or your bed, and includes only a dim lamp or light?

Drs. Kenneth and Rita Dunn's research from St. John's University suggests that the place and conditions you seek out in such a case often reflect which part of the brain you function out of most comfortably.[8] For example, if you learn best in a logical, linear progression and study the parts before you see the whole picture, you probably seek out the quiet, brightly lit, structured sitting area. We call this "left-brain dominance."

If you seek out a learning environment that has some music or other sound, and if you like to sit comfortably or even sprawl on the floor or on your bed with only a little (or soft) light, you may be more of a "right-brain" person. Right-brain people generally see the whole picture quickly and then later realize that it is made up of component parts. They may be more creative individuals. Yes, we can be both. But under stress or a difficult assignment, we generally go to where we are the most comfortable.

Left-Brain Learning Characteristics	Right-Brain Learning Characteristics
1. Logical, linear progression	1. Sees whole picture
2. Parts to whole (deductive reasoning)	2. Whole to parts (inductive reasoning)
3. Analytic	3. Global
4. Factual	4. Intuitive
5. Prefers quiet	5. Prefers some sound
6. Prefers bright light	6. Prefers soft light

7. Learns best alone	7. Learns best as part of a group or in pairs
8. Prefers structured environment (desk or table)	8. Prefers unstructured environment (floor or bed)
Representative Scripture: "Lord, teach us to pray..." (Luke 11:1)	Representative Scripture: "Be still, and know that I am God" (Psalm 46:10)

We have all seen right-brain dominant children who rarely sit up straight in their chairs, preferring to sprawl across a desk. If there's no noise, they create their own by thumping their pencils or tapping their toes. They really do learn best when there's music in the background and they can lie on the floor kicking their legs. At the same time, left-brain dominant children work best when it is quiet and they are seated at a table or desk.

We see examples of both kinds of thinking in the Scriptures. When the disciples asked Jesus to teach them to pray, they were asking him to give them a formula—parts to form a whole. Jesus' response gave them what they were looking for: a model made up of component parts to form the whole prayer.

The Psalms, on the other hand, are nearly all intuitive. We are encouraged to get a sense of the whole picture in many psalms. For example, when we're told in Psalm 46:10 to "be still and *know*" that God is who he says he is, there is no formula to explain how to do that. Knowing God in stillness is a deeply intuitive experience, beyond the grasp of language. Even when you attempt to isolate the component parts, you still come out with less than the whole experience of *knowing* God.

It's important to note that all of us reach into both hemispheres of the brain in the learning process. Some experts have postulated that it is impossible to grasp any truly profound concept or spiritual truth without engaging the right brain. Others have suggested that it is the ability to move fluidly between one hemisphere and the other that leads to the most productive thinking or problem solving.

In considering how these concepts apply to our classrooms, we always come back to our original purpose: to lead our students to Christ and to teach with an eternal focus. The fact is, we may have to lay aside some of our prescribed notions—for example, that children in Sunday school must sit quietly at a table with a bright fluorescent light overhead and finish a work page in order to learn.

Putting It All Together

To help us plan more effectively to reach and teach our learners, let's group the learning patterns we've been discussing into four basic "learner styles." But as we do this, remember: These categories are merely tools to help us get a handle on strategies that will make us more effective teachers of our particular children. No child is going to neatly fit into any one "box."

After all, the Psalms tell us that we are "fearfully and wonderfully made" (Psalm 139:14). God has created each of us as completely unique for his purposes. There are some patterns we may observe among us, but we must never forget that God is a mighty God of infinite variety. In a garden, some flowers bloom in the spring, some in the fall; some need lots of light, some respond better in shade. And so it is with each of us. While we have many things in common, we may need different environments to bloom.

The Looker

- Analytical
- Left-brain dominant
- Visual learner
- Needs to be able to *see* what you are presenting in printed words or pictures
- Important tools: books, pictures, color codes
- Unlikely to be a Control Seeker
- May be an introvert or an extrovert
- Most likely to connect to the Organizer teacher
- **The "Hidden Looker" may be a right-brain artist.**

The Thinker

- Analytical
  - Left-brain dominant
  - Visual or auditory learner
- Needs to sort, classify, and fact-find to *think through* what you are presenting
- Important tools: quiet time, pencil, and paper
- Unlikely to be a Fun Lover
- Usually an introvert
- Most likely to connect to the Researcher teacher
  - **The "Hidden Thinker"** may need to put thoughts into

graphic or word form, which makes him or her appear to be a Looker or a Talker.

The Talker

- Global
- Right-brain dominant
- Auditory learner
- Needs to talk out ideas to *relate to* what you are presenting
- Important tools: discussion, music, word rhythms
- Unlikely to be a Perfectionist
- Extrovert
- Most likely to connect to the Relater teacher
  - **The "Hidden Talker"** may be an introvert who has internal conversations.

The Explorer

- Global
- Right-brain dominant
- Kinesthetic learner
- Needs physical movement or sensory experience to *personally experience* what you are presenting
  - Important tools: own body, movement, models, and toys

- Unlikely to be a Peacemaker
- May be an introvert or extrovert
- Most likely to connect to the Doer teacher
- **The "Hidden Explorer"** may use talking as a form of movement, which makes him or her appear to be a Talker.

Each of these learner styles includes a cluster of characteristics that have been found to commonly go together. Of course, personalities vary within each learner style. The "Hidden Learners" are those we have been fooled by: children who appear to possess one style but can only be opened up with the "keys" of another style.

Throughout this book, we will refer back to both teaching styles and learner styles. In the next chapter, we'll look at specific ways you can learn to build a bridge to specific learner styles at any developmental level.

A Look at Intelligence

When most of us speak of someone as a highly intelligent person, we commonly mean someone who knows a lot or who has the capacity to learn a lot. As individuals, we use some unique criteria to determine what "a lot" is. Early in the twentieth century, psychologists tried to define "a lot" though standardized tests that yielded scores with an average of 100. Anyone with a score over 100 could learn a lot, and everyone with a score below 100 had questionable ability.

In 1983 Howard Gardner, a researcher at Harvard University, published a book titled *Frames of Mind* which detailed his reasons for rejecting those standardized tests as a measure of intelligence. Gardner proposed that intelligence could not be measured by tests that measured only linguistic and mathematical-spatial concepts. While he was not the first to question the numbers applied to intelligence (the intelligence quotient), his particular theory of at least seven distinct types of intelligence has become widely accepted among teachers today.

The types of intelligence that qualified for Gardner's list had to pass through rigorous criteria from the disciplines of culture, history, physiology, and psychology.[9] In revision, he added an eighth intelligence to his list.[10] How Gardner's research applies in a practical way to the classroom is explored by

Dr. Thomas Armstrong in his book, *Multiple Intelligences in the Classroom*.

As Christians, we can see these intelligences reflecting the nature of our infinitely creative God as revealed through Scripture. As teachers, they give us encouragement to use hundreds of different kinds of activities to help our kids become spiritually mature or "God-smart." Any combination of these intelligences can be present within any of the learner styles found on pages 33-35.

Linguistic intelligence—"word smart"

A gift for using languages to understand and express ideas

"In the beginning was the Word, and the Word was with God, and the Word was God" (John 1:1).

Logical-mathematical intelligence—"logic smart"

A gift for seeing cause and effect and manipulating mathematical concepts

"And even the very hairs of your head are all numbered" (Matthew 10:30).

Spatial intelligence—"picture smart"

A gift for making representations of the physical world in one's mind and sometimes for others (such as pictures or sculpture)

"Yet, O Lord, you are our Father. We are the clay, you are the potter; we are all the work of your hand" (Isaiah 64:8).

Bodily-kinesthetic intelligence—"body smart"

A gift for using one's own body (as expressed by athletes and dancers)

"The Lord God formed the man from the dust of the ground and breathed into his nostrils the breath of life, and man became a living being" (Genesis 2:7).

Musical intelligence—"music smart"

A gift for using musical rhythm and tone patterns

"He put a new song in my mouth, a hymn of praise to our God" (Psalm 40:3).

Interpersonal intelligence—"people smart"

A gift for understanding others

"The Lord does not look at the things man looks at. Man looks at the outward appearance, but the Lord looks at the heart" (1 Samuel 16:7).

Intrapersonal intelligence—"self smart"

A gift for understanding one's own inner workings

"Oh, the depth of the riches of the wisdom and knowledge of God! How

unsearchable his judgments, and his paths beyond tracing out! Who has known the mind of the Lord? Or who has been his counselor?" (Romans 11:33-34).

Naturalist intelligence—"nature smart"

A gift for perceiving patterns and classifying, usually in the natural realm, but sometimes in manufactured items, as well

"Now the Lord God had formed out of the ground all the beasts of the field and all the birds of the air. He brought them to the man to see what he would name them; and whatever the man called each living creature, that was its name" (Genesis 2:19).

Reaching All Learners

Deuteronomy 6:6-9 gives us a wonderful biblical basis for reaching out to all types of learners: "These commandments that I give you today are to be upon your hearts. Impress them on your children. *Talk* about them when you sit at home and when you *walk* along the road, when you lie down and when you get up. *Tie* them as symbols on your hands and *bind* them on your foreheads. *Write* them on the doorframes of your houses and on your gates" (author emphasis.)

Let's look at this passage in terms of our learner styles. God wanted the Israelites to internalize his teachings. He presented his Word, stated his goal, and then suggested a variety of methods to accomplish his objective, providing for each learner's style:

• Something to see

"Tie them as *symbols* on your hands and *bind* them on your foreheads. *Write* them on the doorframes of your houses and on your gates" (vv. 8-9, author emphasis).

• Something to talk about

"Talk about them when you sit at home and when you walk along the road, when you lie down and when you get up" (v. 7, author emphasis).

• Something to explore

"Talk about them when you *sit at home* and when you *walk along the road, when you lie down,* and *when you get up"* (v. 7, author emphasis)—in other words, in all the explorations of life.

• Something to think about

"These commandments that I give you today are to be upon your hearts. Impress them on your children" (vv. 6-7).

God wanted his people to be thoughtful about what they transmitted to their children. He wanted them to use every opportunity to bring his commandments into the context of their daily lives. Being a treasured teacher is all about *thoughtfully* and *intentionally* bringing God to children's attention, so that they never forget. The psalmist puts the result of this kind of teaching into a prayer: "Let me understand the teaching of your precepts; then I will meditate on your wonders" (Psalm 119:27).

We teach to the "whole child" because God requires that our love for him emanate from our whole beings. It is this kind of teaching that will support our learners as they fulfill what Jesus said were the two greatest commandments: " 'Love the Lord your God with all your heart and with all your soul and with all your mind and with all your strength. The second is this: 'Love your neighbor as yourself...' " (Mark 12:30-31).

One of the most glorious rewards of teaching is that as we put forth the effort to provide experiences to address our learners' individual needs, our own understanding of God reaches new depths. We discover him in profound richness as we seek to represent him to others, particularly children. The treasured teacher is both a blessing and truly blessed!

Inner Direction

As you think about these questions, make a note of related personal experiences or Scriptures that contribute to your understanding.

1. Which goal of learning (p. 21) do you find yourself spending the most time on? The least? Why?

---

2. Why do you think we retain so little of what we read or hear?

---

3. What's your favorite sense or combination of senses to learn through? What does that tell you about your perceptual strengths?

---

4. Looking back, can you remember a time when you misunderstood a child's developmental level? What happened? What could you have done more effectively?

_____

_____

5. Which learner style best describes your most difficult student? How can you better understand him or her now?

_____

_____

ENDNOTES

1. Thorndike-Barnard Comprehensive Dictionary (Garden City, NY: Doubleday and Company, 1967), 452.
2. "Psychology," Microsoft Corporation: Microsoft Encarta 97 Encyclopedia, 1993-1996.
3. Thom and Joani Schultz, *The Dirt on Learning* (Loveland, CO: Group Publishing, 1999), 155.
4. Adapted from concepts presented in Robert E. Schell, *Developmental Psychology Today* (New York: Random House, Inc., 1983).
5. Adapted from Schell, *Developmental Psychology Today*.
6. Thomas Lickona, *Raising Good Children* (New York: Bantam Books, Inc., 1983), 12.
7. Summarized from James Fowler, *Stages of Faith: The Psychology of Human Development and the Quest for Meaning* (San Francisco: Harper and Row, 1981) and Catherine Stonehouse, *Joining Children on the Spiritual Journey* (Grand Rapids, MI: Baker Books, 1998).
8. Summarized from Kenneth and Rita Dunn, *Bringing Out the Giftedness in Your Child* (New York: John Wiley and Sons, 1992).
9. For detailed information, see chapter 4 of Howard Gardner, *Frames of Mind, Tenth Anniversary Edition* (New York: Basic Books, 1993).
10. Kathy Checkley, "The First Seven...and the Eighth: A Conversation with Howard Gardner." Educational Leadership Online (Volume 55, No. 1). Go to http://www.ascd.org and click on Educational Leadership, then September 1997, "Multiple Intelligences."
11. Thomas Armstrong, *Multiple Intelligences in the Classroom* (Alexandria, VA: Association for Supervision and Curriculum Development, 1994).

Putting Theory
Into Practice

Chapter 3
Building Bridges

Treasured teachers reach beyond their comfort zone to maximize the learning experience for all kinds of learners.

Good composition is like a suspension bridge—
each line adds strength and takes none away.
—Robert Henri, from Donna Ward La Cour,
*Artists in Quotation: A Dictionary of the
Creative Thoughts of Painters, Sculptors,
Designers, Writers, Educators, and Others*

*But in fact God has arranged the parts in the body, every one of them, just
as he wanted them to be. If they were all one part, where would the body be?*
(1 Corinthians 12:18-19)

Our varied styles for taking in, or *perceiving,* information (perceptual strengths), for *processing* information (learning and teaching preferences), and for *personalizing* that information (personality types) are the three factors that combine to form our *patterns* for behaving in learning situations (learner styles). They add remarkable texture to life in the body of Christ. In fact, problems most often arise in our classroom when we don't effectively address individuality in any one of these three arenas or when we give too much attention to any single one of them.

As teachers, we do have a tendency to give a great deal of attention to the style we ourselves possess. Those styles become our teaching habits.

For example, the majority of teachers learn best when they receive information in the visual mode; therefore, much of the traditional teaching process follows a visual track. Visual learners respond positively to this teaching because it is in their comfort zone, too. The success of a majority of students builds positive self-esteem in visual teachers and encourages them to continue to teach in the same way they always have. Thus, the visual-track system of teaching perpetuates itself over the years.

Essentially, we get stuck in a rut that's comfortable for us and for many of our learners. But as 1 Corinthians 12:17 says, "If the whole body were an eye, where would the sense of hearing be?" To be treasured teachers, we must recognize that different students have different ways they learn best—and we must care enough to adapt our teaching style accordingly.

No doubt you've heard the term "paradigm shift," which is used frequently in both the business and education arenas. The word "paradigm" comes from the Greek word *paradignma,* which is a pattern or map for understanding and explaining certain aspects of reality. A paradigm shift comes from making a break with that pattern or map, usually as the result of some new insight. Almost every significant breakthrough in science, business, education or any other arena is the result of someone breaking free from traditional ways of thinking. Many inventions are developed because someone has made a paradigm shift.

A visual teacher's unspoken paradigm may be, "Students learn best when they read along with me and look at pictures." But often, reaching a wide variety of children can occur only when teachers shift their thinking patterns. Almost every successful teacher makes paradigm shifts from time to time.

Sometimes a paradigm shift is small and directed toward a single student— for example, when we identify one of the "Hidden Learners" we met in chapter 2 (p. 35). At other times, a paradigm shift is so significant that it affects our whole lives, as in my breakthrough experience with Johnny (p. 23).

Perhaps in working through chapters1 and 2, you've gotten some insights that are leading you to make your own paradigm shift. Perhaps you'd like to see some of your learners make a paradigm shift. In either case, this chapter will give you some of the tools you need to build bridges between your style and that of your learners—and between who we *are* as teachers and who we would like to *become.* Instead of mindlessly falling into a learning and teaching rut, we can choose to build bridges.

Who Needs a Bridge Anyway?

Consider a teacher who was raised in a very strict, perhaps legalistic school and home environment. By personality, he is a Perfectionist; in teaching style, he is a Researcher. His training has taught him that learning is a very serious thing, and that to be well educated, you must learn in a structured manner.

Now let's say Mr. Perfectionist decides to teach Sunday school to three-year-olds. He brings in all his serious ideas and teaches in a heavily structured way. The children don't relate, and his teaching does not succeed. Because of his perfectionist nature, he determines to try harder—and in accordance with his personality and teaching style, he becomes even more serious and structured. The spiral continues downward as the children relate to him less and less.

How can Mr. Perfectionist break the cycle? He must make a paradigm shift about what teaching should be. He may not be able to change his nature, but his way of thinking about things can be adapted. He can begin to move away from his serious ways and begin to incorporate methods that are more appropriate for three-year olds.

This process is not easy for anyone, especially a very serious, structured Perfectionist-Researcher. Is it possible? Yes, if he is teachable—if he will open himself to new ideas and methods. Is it easy? No, but by the grace of God and with some good tools, he can build a bridge to his three-year-olds. In fact, he can put his Researcher qualities to good use by seeking out information about the most effective ways to teach young kids.

Bridge-building, then, requires six things:

• An *awareness* of the need. Mr. Perfectionist needs to know his own style well enough to perceive a conflict between himself and his three-year-olds. This may take a spark of new insight and understanding about learning and teaching styles.

• A *willingness* to shift strategies from your personal style to the learner's style. Mr. Perfectionist has to be willing to take a step back from what he believes is the way everyone *should* learn and a step toward recognizing the reality of how others *do* learn. Instead of expecting others to adapt to *his* style, he should be willing to be the one who adapts.

• A *mobilization* of your own strengths. Mr. Perfectionist can use his compulsion to succeed to motivate him to seek out new skills. His Researcher style can help him find the information he needs.

• An *effort* to learn new strategies. Mr. Perfectionist is not going to have an immediate understanding about how his young students think. It was his assumption that he knew what three- year-olds needed that got him into trouble in the first place! He will have to try out new teaching tools if he's going to build a bridge.

• An *appreciation* for differences. Mr. Perfectionist has to learn not only to *tolerate* the differences between his style and his learners' styles, but also to express an appreciation for them. They reflect God's creativity and wisdom in putting together the body of Christ.

• A *decision* to teach for the goal. Mr. Perfectionist has to focus on his purpose and mission of reaching and teaching children for Christ and analyze his methods according to how well they produce learning in his students.

While we've "picked on" Mr. Perfectionist, it's obvious that every teacher's style is going to be challenged by some students' individual differences. Even Mrs. Relater, who is ultrasensitive to the needs of her students, may have difficulty with kids who are more structured or aloof.

Bridge-Building Attitudes

Dr. Kathleen Butler, a specialist in learning differences, says that the best way to ensure that you create a bridge to your students is to have a firm grasp of your own teaching style.[1] That style is the reason a student needs a bridge—and it's the anchor point from which you build.

Bridge-building requires a proper attitude that will define the tone of your class and set the stage to help children feel free to discover their own places within the body of Christ. Such an attitude will also help kids learn about the God who loved them enough—exactly the way they are—to send his only Son to reconcile them to himself.

Treasured teachers should strive for a classroom atmosphere that is defined by the following "attitude bridges" we find clearly reflected in Scripture:

• *Be a positive person.* Look for what is *right* about each learner and about the class as a whole. "Finally, brothers, whatever is true, whatever is noble, whatever is right, whatever is pure, whatever is lovely, whatever is admirable—if anything is excellent or praiseworthy—think about such things" (Philippians 4:8).

• *Maintain open communication between yourself and your learners, and among the learners themselves.* Ephesians 4:29 tells us, "Do not let any unwholesome talk come out of your mouths, but only what is helpful for building others up according to their needs, that it may benefit those who listen." Wholesome conversation includes anything that encourages others to be like Christ. It may include God-centered correction. However, it would exclude put-downs, teasing, and dishonesty. In Matthew 5:37, Jesus also spoke of the importance of letting your "yes" be "yes" and your "no" be "no," reminding us again of the importance of simple openness.

• *Create an environment where children can minister to one another.* Our classrooms need to be places where children are encouraged to understand and respond to each other. First Thessalonians 5:14-15 tells us to "warn those who are idle, encourage the timid, help the weak, be patient with everyone. Make sure that nobody pays back wrong for wrong, but always try to be kind to each other and to everyone else." Creating such a positive interpersonal environment may require that you give up old paradigms—for example, the idea that the teacher holds the key to every lesson or that children should keep quiet during class time.

• *Encourage differences.* "We have different gifts, according to the grace given us" (Romans 12:6). Our diversity is part of God's plan and purpose. It isn't enough just to recognize differences; you must really value them and help your students discover how developing their uniqueness can benefit the church.

• *Seek out, respect, and value children's perspectives.* Proverbs 15:22 tells us, "Plans fail for lack of counsel." Seek your students' input as you apply the Word. This will also help you check their perceptions. Help them learn to evaluate their perspectives in light of Scripture.

• *Look for growth and accomplishment.* Let children know that spiritual maturity is a lifelong process. Affirm positive steps along the way, and be confident that their spiritual growth is in the hands of the one who started the work within them—"being confident of this, that he who began a good work in you will carry it on to completion until the day of Christ." (Philippians 1:6).

The goal of incorporating these six attitudes into our classroom is wonderfully articulated in Romans 12:5: "So in Christ we who are many form one body, and each member belongs to all the others."

Bridge-Building to a "Kid Culture"

Treasured teachers often have a gift for understanding children. But even the most gifted among us can be mystified by each new generation of kids. Every few years it seems the "kid culture" changes—what's stylish, what's important, what's in, what's out. Bridge-building must go beyond understanding child development or identifying differences in teaching, learning, and personality styles.

Teachers must seek to understand the "real world" of today's children. How do you do that?

1. Become knowledgeable.

• Read current research. Many popular magazines run regular columns or special sections dealing with children's issues from practical, developmental, and political viewpoints.

• Keep in touch with legislation affecting children and families. These "hot topics" filter down into children's awareness, even when they don't talk about them.

• Pay attention to the community bulletin board features of your local newspaper, parenting papers, and television stations. Know what programs your community is directing toward children.

• Read the background information portions of your teacher guide. These tend to give you age-level appropriate information in small, manageable chunks that are easily applied to your lessons.

• Take time to look at children's school books and textbooks. Ask about the recommended reading list for the age level you teach. Read one of the books they will likely be reading in school.

• Browse the local library or bookstores to find out what issues are being addressed in children's literature.

• Ask kids what issues they and their friends are thinking about.

2. Become a kid watcher.

• Watch children in situations without teachers. Fast-food restaurant play areas are a great place to observe children's interactions with both adults and peers. Parks are another great place for observation.

Because of safety concerns, some parks post signs to prohibit adults who are not accompanied by a child. Be careful to observe in a nonthreatening way, and watch *interactions* rather than individual children.

• Make arrangements to observe kids in other teachers' classrooms, in public schools or day-care centers, or any other place where you are not "in charge." Make it clear that your goal is to watch the children, not to evaluate the teacher. Sometimes you can observe while offering a valuable service to the teacher, like organizing papers or cutting out letters and shapes for a bulletin board.

• Make good use of time spent waiting in lines at the grocery store and elsewhere. Watch interactions between children and caretakers.

• Occasionally attend a child's sporting event to watch how kids interact in a nontraditional learning environment.

3. Become a trend watcher.

• Look for advertising directed toward children; notice the "hook" being used.

• Watch an occasional educational program on television.

• Check out a children's Web site or software.

• Watch Saturday morning cartoons or the Friday night network lineup to find out what kids are seeing on television.

• Take a walk through a toy store or the toy section of a department store.

• Ask kids about their favorite toys or television programs. Ask critical-thinking questions to help you understand their choices, such as

What's the hottest toy at your school?

Why do you think so many kids want...?

What interests you about...?

Would you choose [the main character] as a best friend? Why or why not?

• Ask kids for a review of a new movie or video. Include critical-thinking questions here, as well, such as

Why do you think I should see...?

What did you learn from...?

What do you wish had been left out?

How do you think the characters felt about God?

4. Reach into your own childhood.

• Try to remember how you solved a problem similar to one a student in your class is facing.

• Think about times you felt stressed as a child. Compare the factors to those your students are facing.

• Remember specific things that you enjoyed in a classroom setting similar to yours.

• Recall a time you felt misunderstood by an adult and what you wish that adult had done differently.

• Identify some of the unique things you experienced as a child that affect who you are today. Is there a way to share or replicate those experiences for your learners?

Building a bridge to the "kid culture" depends a great deal on the age of the children involved. It is the natural outgrowth of teaching for age-appropriateness. First, you should know things that the children don't know, things that you will share only in limited fashion (developmental characteristics and management skills, for example). Second, you should have a common body of information you can discuss (what's hot and what's not). Third, you should identify feelings you may have in common to build mutual understanding.

Do you *need* to know about the latest toy or to use "playground talk" in order for kids to understand you? No! But they will appreciate the fact that you have taken an interest in the things that are vying for their attention, and they will respond differently to you than to someone who seems out of touch with their world. Do they have to know what feelings you had as a child? No, but you will relate to them with more compassion as you focus on the commonalties of your feelings.

We've looked at some bridges that apply to all children. Next, we're going to look at some bridges that will help you reach specific learners.

Bridge-Building Language

How we "hear" something that is being communicated to us by a teacher may well be affected by our learner style—whether we're a Looker, a Talker, an Explorer, or a Thinker. For that reason, teachers need to learn the unique "language" that each learner "speaks."

Lookers

Lookers, as a general rule, notice body language. They may hear what your body is saying more than they hear your words. This underscores the need for consistency between our walk and our talk. They respond best to words consistent with their learner style:

- "I am *looking* to *see* who is sitting quietly."
- "I *see* that you found your Bible."
- "*Look* in your Bible to *see* God's *view* of obeying your parents."

Body language. Lookers respond positively to visual body language clues. Smile. Use direct eye contact. Adopt body language that communicates love and joy rather than anger and frustration. Lookers may pick up on tense body cues that are left over from, say, your struggle to get out of the house on time that morning, and they may wonder, "Is the teacher upset with me?"

Environmental communication. Lookers like their learning environment to be orderly and attractive. They notice when the teacher brings order and creativity to the classroom. As a teacher who is a Looker, I personally look for ways to make my classroom as attractive as possible. Some children seem oblivious to this, but Lookers always respond positively to changes and additions to the physical environment. In fact, they often have very strong reactions to their environment and may respond to it unconsciously with their behavior. Respect and protect this unique characteristic, even as you work to train Lookers in tolerance and adaptability.

My son is a Looker and notices when I have done something to his bedroom. He spends time working on his room to get it just the way he likes it. I must admit, he takes after me. As a Looker, I have to have my physical environment just the way I like it before I can concentrate. I also need quiet. At one time, a piano teacher conducted lessons in the room right next to my office. I love music, but I quickly learned I could not work effectively with sound distractions. I learned to do things on piano-lesson day that did not require concentration, like purchasing supplies and cleaning the resource room.

Talkers

Talkers have to check their perceptions frequently through verbalizing their thoughts and gaining your feedback. They respond well to words that are consistent with their learner style:

- "I *hear* what you are *saying.*"
- "I am *listening* for people who are remembering our rules."
- "It *sounds* as though you really understand that!"

Body language. Talkers hear the slightest change in your verbal communication. They pick up on irritation or indecision in your voice and may take advantage of it or become unsettled by it. A paradox with these learners is that they process what they are learning not merely by hearing but also by talking about it. But while Talkers often generate noise, they do not respond well to noise from others because it gets in the way of their hearing and forming their own thoughts into words.

Environmental communication. Talkers like to have some sound in the environment and will sometimes create it—humming or toe-tapping, for example. Providing "white noise," such as soft classical music, may help them focus. Even sitting them near something that hums, like an air-conditioning unit or a computer, can do the trick. Give them frequent opportunities to share their thoughts with others.

My oldest son is a Talker. He likes to study with music in the background. He often talks loudly and more frequently than many would like, yet he is intolerant of noise created by others. When the dog barks or his siblings play the piano, he is the first to be distracted. The challenge is to help him learn tolerance of others while not creating so much noise himself.

Explorers

Explorers need physical touch, and they respond to fewer words than Lookers and Talkers. Words that Explorers do "hear" include

- "I am *touched* by what you said."
- "*Hold* that thought, and we will discuss it some more."
- "I'm looking for people who are *doing* the right thing."
- "Do you have a *grip* on what I've asked you to do?"

Body language. Touch is definitely the arena in which you reach Explorers, although you have to be particularly sensitive to the appropriateness of how you touch. Frequently passing by these children or standing near them helps a great deal. Love pats on the head or arm encourage them, and a firm but gentle hand on the shoulder can help keep them in line. The more things you can give Explorers to do, the more you can effectively direct their busy bodies. Let these children collect papers, pass out markers, erase the board, and do any other appropriate tasks you can think of.

Because these children need touch to such a great extent, Explorers have trouble keeping their hands off others. They need constant reminders, like "We keep our hands and feet to ourselves." The best way to avoid problems is to have something in Explorers' hands as often as possible to keep them occupied. I prefer to give them something that doesn't make noise, such as a piece of masking tape, a ribbon, a cotton ball, a chenille wire, or a small lump of clay. Some Explorers can be occupied by chewing gum.

Environmental communication. Having things in the classroom that children can touch is an emotional security blanket for Explorers. Because they are always "fiddling," Explorers often receive the message that they are annoying others. This can be frustrating, since they don't understand why they do what they do. Give them appropriate ways to channel touch and movement in order to learn.

Once I substituted in a class where there was nothing for the children to touch. I noticed that one little boy in particular—a definite Explorer—was a constant distraction to the rest of the children. I handled this by sitting him next to me. I patted and touched him frequently and allowed him to play with my hand. As I got ready to present the Gospel message, I took off my necklace and gave it to him to touch. The teaching went smoothly, and every child had an opportunity to hear about Jesus that day.

As Explorers grow up, we can help them understand their need for touch and give them appropriate ways to accommodate this when there is nothing offered in the environment. Instead of "fiddling," for example, Explorers can be encouraged to doodle or fold paper or substitute small muscle movements for moving their entire bodies.

Thinkers

Thinkers often appear to be in their own worlds, and when they come out, it is often to argue or disagree with what you've said! They don't believe they are really learning unless they are being presented with facts, figures, or objective information. Because they are the most linear of all your learners, they respond well to words that relate to their sense of precision and order:

- *"How many* disciples were there?"
- *"When and where* was Jesus crucified?"
- *"First,* I'd like you to get your crayons. *Next,* draw your picture. *Then* show me what you've done."
- "I'm *waiting* for you to *think it through."*
- "You have *two minutes* to finish."

Body language. Thinkers respond well to respect for their personal space. They often appreciate private rather than public recognition. Eye contact and nods of approval demonstrate your respect for their contributions. They are more affirmed by gestures such as a wink or a thumbs-up than by a touch (although sometimes you can slip in a "high-five" from a distance).

Environmental communication. Thinkers appreciate order in their environment. Displays of factual information, such as charts and lists, as well as the availability of documentation or resource material, make them feel comfortable. Thinkers often appreciate lecture followed by a quiet time to think things through as well as an opportunity to demonstrate their understanding. They may even enjoy taking a written test at the end of each class session!

Whenever possible, give Thinkers opportunities to figure out problems or write answers on a chalkboard. Offer them time during class to do something on their own. Don't insist that Thinkers always participate in a group or always share their conclusions—although it is important to teach them to cooperate and value the contributions of others.

Bridge-Building Activities

Proper attitudes, effective culture-bridging, and attention to language are the "soft" things that build a bridge from your teaching style to your student's learner style. Specific activities and what I call "thought-provokers" are the "hard," more tangible elements that you use in the process.

As you become more experienced in teaching to reach a variety of learners, you will no doubt come up with all kinds of specific activities that will make your classroom an effective learning environment. The following "activity bridges," which are broadly categorized according to the learner style they will appeal to, can help you get started. Fill in the blanks to tailor the activities to your lesson content. Many ideas listed for one learner style would also be quite appropriate for others.

Bridges to the Looker

Directive words:

Draw	Sculpt	Color code
Design	Make a collage	Highlight
Illustrate	Diagram	Match
Write	Paint	Cartoon

Activity starters:

Find a picture that reminds you of…

Do a photo essay about...

Draw the expression on [name]'s face when...

Arrange these objects to show...

Create a T-shirt design to represent...

Make a costume for...

Choose a color to represent...

Position people to show...

Set up a display window for...

Watch a video segment without the sound, and decide how what's happening relates to the lesson about...

Make a picture outline of...

Draw this verse in picture form (rebus).

Create a trading card for...(a Bible character, a fruit of the Spirit, each of the plagues of Egypt)

Design a symbol or logo for...

Write and illustrate a children's book about...

Make a transparency of..., then project it onto the wall

Create a book cover for the book of...(Genesis, Psalms, John)

Design a modern home for...(Adam, Moses, Paul)

Sculpt a statue in honor of...

Create one item to hang on a mobile for each part of the story of...

My activities for Lookers:

_____

_____

_____

Tools to provide:

Art supplies

Posters

Picture books

Posted rules

Written directions

Visual tokens of appreciation and affirmation (stickers, stamps, happy faces, displays of their work)

Bridges to the Talker

Directive words:

Share	Write a script	Ask
Say	Sing	Tell
Discuss	Make up a chant or rhyme	Whisper
Compose	Interview	Mouth the words

Activity starters:

What song reminds you of...?

Write a puppet skit about the conversation between...

What do you think [name] might have wanted to say when...

Talk about _____ for one minute without stopping.

Say everything you know about _____ before I ring the bell.

Summarize the message of the story of _____ for a bumper sticker.

Write a song about _____ to the tune of a familiar nursery rhyme.

What words describe _____ (a Bible character, a place, an event)?

What tone of voice do you think [name] used when he...?

Choose background music for...

Pretend you are [name], and describe your feelings when...

What sounds do you think [name] heard as...?

What would you like to say to...?

What questions would you like to ask each character in the Bible story?

Make a tape interviewing...

Create sound effects while someone reads the story aloud.

Plan a news report from...(the location of the story).

What would you like to teach [name]?

What do you think God would say about...?

Pretend you are a lawyer. Make your opening argument for...

My activities for Talkers:

_____

_____

_____

Tools to provide:

Cooperative projects/peer interaction

Discussion questions

Tape recorder

Tape player or CD player and music

Frequent oral review of rules and directions (Let them restate the rules.)

Verbal affirmation and feedback (applause, "Good job," repeat their conclusions, restate what you heard them say, public recognition)

Bridges to the Explorer

Directive words:

Experiment with	Find	Stand by
Act out	Act like	Arrange
Feel	Move	Rearrange
Touch	Do	Play with

Activity starters:

Touch something in the room that reminds you of…

Create a moving figure to represent…

Come up with a game that shows…

Make a snack that…

What sport best illustrates…? Why?

Use these toys to re-create…

Move the furniture so that the classroom is like…

Move your body like [name] did when…

Role play…

Make your face look like [name]'s did when…

Build a model of…

Repeat one (word of the verse, important idea) each time you (catch the ball, take a step).

Create a different action for each detail of the story about… Retell the story without words.

Create motions to help you remember this Bible verse…

Find props to use for the story of… (Make sure everyone gets to handle them.)

Play charades to express this concept…

Act out exaggerated details of the story about… (For example, imagine what the sand must have felt like against the Israelites' feet, and move as you imagine they did.)

Work as a group to form...(Noah's ark, the stormy sea, the Ten Commandments).

Do this experiment... How is it like...

My activities for Explorers:

_____

_____

_____

Tools to provide:

Open space

Three-dimensional art and building supplies

Sports equipment

Multisensory items (interesting textures and substances, sticky or magnetic objects, cooking projects)

Time to create

Tangible rewards and affirmation (free time, pizza party, hugs, enthusiastic praise)

Bridges to the Thinker

Directive words:

Group	Graph	Analyze
List	Chart	Figure out
Categorize	Organize	Recite
Map	Plan	Memorize

Activity starters:

Use the map to determine...(two different possible routes, the distance between...).

Use the map to determine what modern countries now occupy the lands of these biblical nations: ...

How is _____ like_____?

List all the _____mentioned in this Scripture passage.

Find five times Jesus mentioned...

Put the events of…(Christmas, Jesus' last week, David's life) in chronological order.

Make a time line to show…

Gather evidence to defend…

List the events that led to…

What might happen if [name] did the same thing today?

Tell three things that were wrong about…

Compare these two similar Scripture passages or Bible stories: …

Write a set of rules or directions for…(certain biblical characters or groups).

What was [name's] biggest mistake?

How are you like [name]? How are you different?

Name all the…

What happened as a result of…?

How many times did…?

What questions would you have asked if you were…?

My activities for Thinkers:

Tools to provide:

Additional information and interesting "tidbits" to connect the Bible to life

Resource materials and reference books

Maps

Charts comparing Bible data

Opportunities for ongoing projects

Affirmation by recognizing expertise and specific contributions, providing opportunities for in-depth study, using and applying the Thinker's knowledge

Inner Direction

As you think about these questions, make a note of related personal experiences or Scriptures that contribute to your understanding:

1. How do you see your teaching style affecting the Looker? the Talker? the Explorer? the Thinker?

_____

_____

2. Think about your most memorable treasured teacher. What bridges did he or she build to you?

_____

_____

3. In what areas are you currently building effective bridges to your students?

_____

_____

4. Which area do you see as being most difficult for you to bridge with your students? Why?

_____

_____

5. What is your most recent paradigm shift? How do you see that shift impacting your teaching?

_____

_____

ENDNOTE

1. Kathleen Butler, *It's All in Your Mind: A Student's Guide to Learning Style* (Columbia, CT: The Learner's Dimension, 1988).

Chapter 4
PLAY-ful Planning

*Treasured teachers know the importance of proper
planning and commit time to preparing thoroughly.*

Christians ought to be the strongest, broadest, most creative
thinkers in the world...In Christ there is a foundation
of truth that ought to make our ideas, our analysis of things,
and our innovations among the most powerful of the age.
—Gordon MacDonald, *Ordering Your Private World*

*"The plans of the diligent lead surely to advantage, but everyone who is hasty
comes surely to poverty"* (Proverbs 21:5, New American Standard)

The mark of a treasured teacher is not so much the ability to impart information but a contagious enthusiasm for learning. That excitement and eagerness are especially important when it's time to plan the lesson for next week's Sunday school class. Preparation is critical. Even the most experienced among us must be continually planning and learning new things to impart to our kids.

Of course, time is a precious commodity for all of us. I can't tell you how many times I've been asked by new teachers, "How long will it take me to prepare my lesson each week?" In this chapter I want to show you how to prepare lessons in the simplest way possible. I also want to show you how to sink your "spiritual roots" deeply so that your Bible lessons transform your students.

I won't kid you: It will take time. And it will take a new teacher more time than it will take an experienced teacher. God grows us into the job. But if we sow "quick-fix preparation," our lessons will reap only shallow teaching and superficial life application. We live in a society that wants "instant everything." But if that is how we prepare to teach God's Word, our work will not bear fruit.

Planning doesn't have to be drudgery! Several years ago, Robert Fulghum captured our hearts with his book of short essays, *All I Really Need to Know I Learned in Kindergarten : Uncommon Thoughts on Common Things.*[1] Fulghum reminded us that much of our lifelong learning is done informally, through the work we call "play." Since lifelong learning is what we're after each time we teach lessons from God's Word, it seems appropriate to use the letters of the word "play" to remind us of the elements of our preparation.

P—Pray and ponder the passage.

Prayer is where our teaching should always originate. In fact, prayer is so important in a teacher's life that we will devote the whole next chapter to its significance. But let's look at it as an element of lesson preparation here.

Why is prayer part of effective planning? Because prayer links us with our Heavenly Father, giving us access to his wisdom as well as guidance from the Holy Spirit. Through prayer, we *see* his vision, *hear* his heart, *touch* the significance of the lesson, and attempt to *think* his thoughts.

For whom do you pray? For your students, of course! Pray first for their salvation. Then pray for them to continue to grow in Jesus, to become disciples of Christ who hunger to know him and his Word. Pray for them to become people who shine the light of Jesus into the world. Pray also for their hearts to be prepared for the message God has for them during this particular lesson. Pray for their individual needs, as well.

What do you pray? Pray that God would open your understanding of his Word so that you are enabled to teach your lesson in a way that transforms the lives of your students. Pray that with God's help you can encourage your students to want to change and to seek out God's Word to make that change.

Along with prayer, ponder the lesson's Scripture passage in the presence of God. Allow the Holy Spirit to permeate your thoughts so that you might deeply experience the significance of this particular verse, perhaps reading it from several different translations to expand your opportunity for in-depth understanding. Invite God to give you deep insight into his Word so that it becomes living and active in your own life. Seek God's blessing on the rest of your preparation, making sure that every activity will honor him.

It is usually easy to spot those treasured teachers who have bathed their students and their teaching in prayer. There is a special bond that forms between the teacher and the children in those classes, and you sense the sweet presence of the Holy Spirit when you walk into the room. Clearly, the teaching is being applied to those young lives through the work of the Holy Spirit. How I love to encourage teachers to make prayer the springboard for their teaching!

After we have built the foundation for our lesson in prayer, we are ready to move on to preparing the lesson through study.

L—Learn the lesson.

The learning phase of lesson planning is when we seek answers to the intellectual questions we may have encountered as we prayed and pondered the lesson's Scripture passage. Some teaching styles may actually integrate this phase of planning into the "pondering" phase. Analytical-style teachers (Researchers and Organizers) may feel more comfortable looking at the parts of a passage before they seek a "global perspective" in prayer. The order of the elements is not nearly as important as the fact that we choose to seek God's wisdom in understanding both the big picture and the parts of our Bible teaching.

As you study the Bible passage eagerly, personally, and thoughtfully, seek to answer the following questions:

• *Who?* Who is the passage about? To whom was this person (or persons) connected? What was happening at this time in his or her life? To whom was the passage originally directed? Under what circumstances was it written?

• *What?* What is the main point of this passage? What can you (or your students) learn from this passage that would make a difference in your life today?

• *Where?* Where does this verse fall in the context of the whole chapter, or the whole book? Does the geography of its setting have any significance? Where would this passage have practical application to modern life?

• *When?* When was this passage written? Are there specific, predictable times in life when this passage could be especially significant?

• *Why?* Why is this passage important for us to consider today? Why is it important for your students to understand this passage?

This is the point in preparation where we might use Bible reference materials, such as commentaries, Bible dictionaries, Bible handbooks, maps, or a concordance, to find related Scriptures. These tools add depth to our understanding of the lesson. Once we are comfortable with our background knowledge (remember, your style will determine your comfort level in this area), we are ready to get into the practical aspects of planning for our particular class.

A—Analyze your aids.

Look carefully and somewhat critically at your curriculum guide. What teaching aids does it provide? Look at each portion of the lesson, and decide if it meets the needs of your students. Then you're ready for the next steps.

• *Synthesize for a single focus.*

After considering all you've learned from praying and studying about the teaching passage and after adding all you know about your students' lives (including their developmental levels and unique circumstances), ask yourself: What's the single most important thing they could learn from this lesson? It is more important for students to leave with one thought they will remember and apply than with four or five ideas they can't really put a finger on. This single focus will provide structure for the remainder of your planning.

If your curriculum has not already identified a single focus, make sure you formulate a clear and concise statement yourself. Use the simple language of your children rather than the formal grammar of a theologian—for example, "God wants us to be kind" or "Jesus heals sick people" or "God gives us help through good friendships."

• *Search for sensory connections.*

Review the Bible passage thinking about what sensory images it evokes. Are there words in the story that make you think of taste ("Your words are sweeter than honey…")? smell (the burning sacrifices)? sight (the rainbow of promise)? touch (the cool wash water on the feet of the disciples)? hearing (the roar of rushing wind)? Develop at least one activity that provides a sensory connection to the Scripture passage. In general, the younger the students, the more important the sensory connections.

• *Strategize for style.*

Look at the tone of the lesson, and consider how recommended activities in the teacher guide cater to specific learner styles. How can your sensitivity to learner styles improve this lesson? Are Looker-, Talker-, Explorer-, and Thinker-type questions included for you to use? Highlight them, or write your own questions in the margins of your book.

Next, think about your room arrangement. Is it conducive to teaching this lesson? Could parts of the lesson be more effectively taught in dim light or in the dark? Is this a story that is better taught on a blanket than at a table? Would arranging to go outside be appropriate?

Ask: What learner styles are being catered to this week? Is it the same configuration of styles that were addressed last week? It isn't realistic to expect to have a full activity specifically directed to each learner style each week, but you can make sure you integrate options and questions that address each learner's needs somewhere in every lesson. (Use the "activity bridges" on p. 53 for ideas.)

• *Search out supplies.*

The easiest way for me to think through a supply list (even if one is provided in the teacher guide) is to fold a piece of paper into thirds. I list things I know are in my classroom in the first column, things I know I have around the house in the second column, and things I will have to purchase or otherwise acquire in the third column. Then I make sure I have all those supplies in one place before class time. More good lessons go wrong because of teachers having to struggle to get their hands on the right supplies than for any other reason I know!

When I teach in early childhood classes, I always seem to have a million supplies for each craft or activity. To keep organized, I often use plastic shoe boxes with lids, filling one for each activity and stacking them in order of their use. I also color-code them so I don't get confused! If I need the same supply for two activities (glue, for example), I simply put the items into the second bin when I clean up from the first activity. This strategy works great for centers, too. (More about centers in chapter 9.)

Another idea is to find a box that has dividers (such as the kind used for shipping glass items). You can put one type of supply in each of the divided sections, or put all of the portioned supplies for each child in a separate divider. This saves so much hassle!

Once we've gone through these practical steps, it's time to bring our planning full circle and evaluate our personal readiness.

Y—Yield Yourself to Be Used

Teaching God's Word is a process that involves the divine teacher, the Holy Spirit, seeking to teach through human teachers—you and me. We need to practice teaching our lesson so we become comfortable with the information. This doesn't mean that we go through every aspect with a live audience, but it does mean we review the material a few times.

Teachers who are Lookers process the lesson best when they write out what they are going to do. Talkers often need to discuss it. Explorers need to do something to internalize the lesson. We must work with our strengths as we prepare. The more comfortable we are with the material, the more likely we are to have a positive experience.

But it is not enough to simply prepare to teach. We must prepare to *be*. To paraphrase James 1:22, we must be doers of the Word and not teachers only! We have to look at our lesson plan much as a traveler would view a road map, a cook would refer to a recipe, or an architect would rely on blueprint. It is a guide to help us get to where we want to be. But even a careful preparation of material will be useless unless we have carefully prepared our lives as well.

Before you teach, ask yourself:

• *Does my walk match my talk?* Is there consistency between what I am teaching my students and what I am attempting to live in my own life?

• *Have I confessed the known sins in my life and asked God to reveal to me those of which I am unaware?* We all have blind spots. When we ask God to give us a window into our own weaknesses and sins, it can often be painful—but it's necessary!

• *Am I sinking my spiritual roots deeply?* The more time we invest in studying the Bible, praying, and then applying God's truth to our own lives, the more effectively we can teach others.

• *Am I growing in my own spiritual life?* That's the bottom line. It adds authenticity to our teaching when we can say, "Look what the Lord taught me this week with this passage." Nothing teaches more effectively than authenticity backed up with enthusiasm.

Elements of an Effective Hour

The goal of all of our planning is to provide an effective learning experience—to teach a lesson our students will learn and remember and respond to by applying the message to their lives. Thom and Joani Schultz, authors of *The Dirt on Learning,* use the term "authentic learning" to describe this.[2]

Authentic learning is built on these characteristics:

• *It is learner-focused.* No matter how well-prepared and knowledgeable teachers are, it doesn't really mean much unless learners learn. Our individual teaching strengths will impact our perspectives, but the needs of our learners must determine our approach.

• *It takes a thinking approach.* Critical thinking skills are important to encourage at any age. We should require our students to recall facts and figures only as a gateway for questions that probe real life applications.

• *It involves active learning.* Active learning encourages experiences that touch all learner styles because individual learners are able to perceive and process the experience in their own unique ways. While some activities may be geared to particularly grab one learner style or intelligence, each activity is valuable for the whole group's understanding. By "debriefing" the students—guiding conversation in a way that encourages them to apply the experience to their lives—we can heighten the impact.

• *It includes interactive learning.* Learners need opportunities to share their perspectives with others. We can encourage interaction by allowing learners to verbalize their thoughts, have conversations, participate in group discussions, work together cooperatively, and try out each other's ideas. All interactive learning has a learner-to-learner component.

To help ensure authentic teaching, each lesson you plan should include the five E's: Engage, Explore, Expand and Express, and Evaluate. Most likely, these elements are addressed in some way in your teacher guide, although each curriculum may express them a bit differently. Whether or not they are listed for you, it is still wise to write them out for your own purposes.

1. Engage

As children first arrive in the classroom, you should engage them by providing some presession activities. These can be related to the lesson or may simply be focused upon a particular task. The idea is to avoid random behavior that often leads to discipline problems.

Often churches have a break between the Sunday school hour and the worship service hour, but the children stay in their classrooms. The first-hour teacher may be cleaning up while the second-hour teacher is wanting to set up. This can cause confusion and a lack of structure that some children respond to with discipline problems. Your presession activities are invaluable during this time.

I wish every teacher could have observed one of the teachers I worked with; I'll call him Mr. Carlton. He always got to his classroom early and had at least ten interesting things for the children to do as they arrived. He had paper on the wall for drawing, clay for creating, puzzles to assemble, pictures to color, felt board lessons for kids to do on their own, games he had recycled from his old resource packets—a veritable haven for the child on the move! The children entered his room with excitement and curiosity, wondering what treasures awaited them that day. If only we could clone the Mr. Carltons of the world!

Once all your children have arrived, gather them together to do something of high interest that will focus them on the single point you want to teach—and get their minds off the fact that they got up late or had a hard time finding matching socks. Through this "engage activity," you get the kids to "sign up" for the rest of the lesson.

You also lead them into an awareness of their need. Here's what I mean. Let's say you are teaching a lesson about the good Samaritan. Your engage activity might be a game in which the children are on their way to a goal (say, moving from one part of the room to another) and something or someone gets in their way. They have to either deal with the obstacle, push it aside, or go around it. As a result, they have the opportunity to actually experience what it feels like to encounter an obstacle when they are focused on a goal—much like the characters in the story of the good Samaritan, who were so focused on their goals that they forgot what was really important and failed to stop and help someone in need.

Children who hear this story often seem sure that they would be like the good Samaritan in a similar situation and would stop to help a person in trouble. They don't recognize the behavior of the priest or Levite in themselves, nor do they see their own need to work more diligently at caring for their neighbors. I've seen those same "Samaritans" go out and knock each other flat on the playground to get to the slide or swings first—without noticing the correlation between their behavior and what they just learned in class. But once children, through the engage activity, have been led to see that they, too, are tempted to avoid or ignore an obstacle when it is in the way of their goal, their hearts are prepared for the good Samaritan's message.

After such an active experience, you can ask open-ended questions that will help kids identify themselves when you read the Bible story later—for example,

• What went through your mind when you first saw the obstacle?

• What did you choose to do with the obstacle?

• When has something like this happened to you in real life? Were you stopped by the obstacle, or did you rush past it?

We have to meet students where they live in terms of their own life experiences. Often children see a Bible story as having happened long ago and thus having no relevance to their own situation. It is our job as teachers to help them see that our hearts have not changed since Bible times. We all struggle with sinful attitudes and behaviors. The "sin nature" may manifest itself in different ways, but it's there, just the same.

Remember, at this point the Bible story itself has not been introduced—only the need situation presented in the story. And while the kids are absorbed in the significance of the human conflict, you can move on to the exciting part!

2. Explore

This is when you go to the Bible to discover what God has to say about the need that's been expressed. Each lesson must make this transition clear: When we have a need, we go to God's Word to see what to do about it!

Read the Bible story out loud, using a clear voice and lots of inflection. Make it sound as though you are really excited by the content—as though you can hardly wait to get to the next phrase. Be expressive, reading the way someone would actually say the words if they were speaking them.

Have the children follow along with their fingers in their own Bibles. If your students use several translations, it may be wise to write out the passage and make copies so that they can follow along in the same version. It's a little extra work, but it keeps everyone focused on the same words.

Yes, it is wonderful to ask students to read aloud. But I believe the main reading of the passage needs to be done in the clearest way possible. If the students each read a verse, they often use different translations, speak at different volumes, and sometimes stumble over the words. The result is that they don't get the benefit of hearing the Scripture read clearly and expressively as a unit, and the passage loses its continuity. Look for other opportunities for children to read the Bible out loud—not now.

I also believe teachers should teach with their Bibles open. Whatever tools you are using, place them inside your Bible so the students can see that it is God's Word you are teaching from. After all, you are trying to instill in your students the habit of going to God's Word. The best way to do that is through modeling.

I like to write notes in my Bible with a red pencil. (Must be the teacher in me!) One day a playful child saw my notes and said, "Hey, what's black and white and red all over? Mrs. Capehart's Bible!" Then he stopped short and looked at me, afraid that I would be upset at his joke. I only smiled. I want my students to *want* to look at my Bible and see a book well used and greatly loved. My Bible is like an old friend!

Of course, it's important for children to get experience in actually using their own Bibles. If we want to have our students go to the Word of God for wisdom in dealing with life issues, we need to train them how to do it. *The Ultimate Bible Handbook for Children's Ministry* [3] recommends many activities to help children make God's Word their own "best friend." Here are a few guidelines:

• Show children how to divide the Bible in half with their thumbs and then to divide the section on the right once again in order to get close to the New Testament. A few practices with this will enable them to find their way quickly to the Gospels.

• Teach children the books of the Bible in order. Child Evangelism Fellowship has a wonderful song and visuals to do this. (Check the bibliography for information about contacting CEF).

• Give students opportunities to practice looking up Scriptures without time pressure. You might pair the children up or direct them to work in groups. Be patient; remember, there are many *adults* who can't find their way around the Bible! The more comfortable and successful kids feel in doing something, the more apt they are to do it. Success breeds success. Let's grow children who are comfortable with the Word of God.

During the "explore" phase of the lesson, it's important to include activities that bring the Bible to life. Look for ways to integrate your knowledge of learner styles here and to offer experiences that will encourage authentic learning.

3. Expand and express

Once your students have had a chance to explore both the human and scriptural perspectives of the lesson, you can help them begin to make life-applications. While the children may have been connecting the teaching to themselves all along the way, this is their opportunity to let the concepts take root.

This is the "do" part of the lesson. In the context of the lesson about the good Samaritan, a Looker-oriented project might be to draw and color a picture of the roadside scene. A Talker-oriented project might be to divide into discussion groups and plan a service project to show concern for others. An Explorer-oriented project might be to stage a re-enactment of the story. A Thinker-oriented project might be to search newspapers or magazines for "good

Samaritan" stories or to research the origins of "Good Samaritan" laws.

It's not enough to stop there, though. Each lesson should call all students to formulate a plan of action for expressing the truth of the lesson in their own lives. You can stimulate this kind of thinking by asking questions, such as

• When were you too busy to help someone who needed you? What will you do the next time?

• Who will you care for this week? How will you explain to them why you want to help?

• Are there people like the man who was robbed in your neighborhood, in your church, in your class at school? How do you think God wants you to respond to those people this week?

Another effective way to encourage self-awareness in your students is to share from your own life experience. What opportunities have you had to apply the lesson of the good Samaritan? Sharing from your heart can serve as a catalyst to get them thinking and examining their own hearts in the light of God's Word.

The "expand and express" portion of the lesson can also lead to prayer. This should be a high point of your lesson time, communicating to the kids that they are not on their own as they seek to apply the truths they have learned. Learning to pray with others is one of the great privileges of the Christian life. During prayer, children can express their care, concern, and support for one another. And if you help keep the prayer directed by the same single focus of the lesson, it can be a powerful learning experience, too. (For ideas about how to make prayer meaningful for children, see chapter 5.)

4. Evaluate

A planned evaluation time can be one of the most important aspects of your lesson, offering students the opportunity to review and synthesize what they have learned. It can also give you important feedback about the kinds of activities that reach your unique learners—information that will help you in future planning.

When I do this phase, I like to briefly go over each activity from the lesson, highlighting interesting observations the children made throughout the class time. This affirmation of their contributions says to them, "You have a significant place in the body of Christ. " If we haven't prayed yet, I find that this is a good time to pray and "commission" the children to put the lesson into practice.

After the children leave, it is important that you continue the evaluation. Ask yourself:

- What went well?
- What would I do differently if I taught the lesson again?
- What can I watch for in my students' behaviors that will let me know they really learned the lesson?
- What follow-up questions can I ask in the next class session to reinforce what was taught today? (You'll especially want to ask them how they applied the lesson during the week!)

As you carry out your evaluation phase, seek to have an *eternal focus*. We must never think of teaching God's Word as just one more thing to check off our "To Do" list for the week. Remember, you are investing your time in a purpose that impacts eternity. In today's transient society, it's possible that you'll see the kids move before you see them grow up. You may never witness the tangible results of your teaching. But the most significant thing you can do for a family is to lead their child to Christ. Trust God to do the rest.

Inner Direction

As you think about these questions, make a note of related personal experiences or Scriptures that contribute to your understanding:

1. Consider this poem by an unknown author. What does it mean to you?

Dear Lord, I do not ask
That Thou shoulds't give me
Some high work of Thine,
Some noble calling, or some wondrous task.
Give me a little hand to hold in mine,
Give me a little child to point the ways:
Over the strange, sweet path that leads to Thee;
Give me a little voice to teach to pray;
Give me two shining eyes Thy face to see.
The only crown I ask, dear Lord, to wear is this:
That I may teach a little child.

I do not ask that I may ever stand
Among the wise, the worthy, or the great;
I only ask that softly, hand in hand,
A child and I may enter at the gate.

2. In which area of "Play-ful Planning" do you excel? Which area is a challenge?

_____

_____

3. In what ways can understanding and using your own personal style make planning more inviting for you?

_____

_____

4. What rewards have you observed from careful preparation? What have you observed when your planning is less than thorough?

_____

_____

5. How does your curriculum address the five E's? What do you have to add to make sure each lesson is well rounded?

_____

_____

ENDNOTES

1. Robert Fulghum, *All I Really Need to Know I Learned in Kindergarten: Uncommon Thoughts on Common Things* (New York, NY: Ivy Books, 1988).
2. Thom and Joani Schultz, "Authentic Learning," Children's Ministry (July/August 1998), 22.
3. *The Ultimate Bible Handbook for Children's Ministry* (Loveland, CO: Group Publishing, 1999).

Chapter 5
Powerful Praying

Treasured teachers trust in the power of prayer and regard praying for their students as a God-given privilege.

Our prayers are the link between God's
inexhaustible resources and people's needs.
—Charles Stanley, *Handle With Prayer*

*"Be anxious for nothing, but in everything by prayer and supplication
with thanksgiving let your requests be made known to God"*
(Philippians 4:6, New American Standard).

P rayer is an adventure—a life-creating, life-changing journey into a closer relationship with God. As Richard Foster writes in *Celebration of Discipline,* "Prayer catapults us onto the frontier of the spiritual life." [1] All who have accomplished great things for God have experienced prayer as the main pursuit of their lives. Martin Luther said, "I have so much business I cannot get on without spending three hours daily in prayer." [2]

Prayer is the main avenue God uses to guide and change our lives. As important as prayer is, however, there is something that undergirds it: our relationship with God. No teaching method, no degree of skill, no amount of commitment or energy, not even the act of prayer itself, will accomplish God's goals for his learners. It is the relationship and intervention of God in the lives of his people that effects change. As church leader and author Henry Blackaby has explained, "*It* never works! *He* works! The method is never the key to accomplishing God's purposes. The key is your relationship to a Person." [3] Prayer is how we develop that relationship.

I think most of us understand that prayer is important, and as teachers we sense the need to pray more for our students. But too often, we don't follow through. What prevents us from practicing what we know to be right and true?

Prayer, I believe, is a battle each of us faces. A prayer warrior in our church once told me that he underwent a battle every morning before he finally got up and got praying. When we realize that prayer is a battle, we can learn how to win.

Our students learn far more from *who* we *are* than from *what we say,* and who we are is determined largely by our commitment to prayer. This chapter will suggest practical tools to help you win your personal prayer battle as well as to lead your children into meaningful prayer experiences.

A Personal Journey

One treasured teacher described to me how her own conviction to pray for her students developed after she became a department leader.

"I noticed that one teacher in the primary department came early every Sunday morning. She went into her classroom and quietly prayed. One day, as I delivered the take-home lessons, I saw her praying through a set of note cards. It aroused my curiosity. She said she kept a card for each student on which she wrote prayer requests, and this helped her to pray specifically for her students each week. The difference in her class was obvious. What a testimony to prayer this woman was!

"I began to do the same for my own class. I arrived five minutes early to 'bathe the room in prayer.' I began to notice a difference. After a few weeks, I wrote a note card for a student that I knew was going through a divorce at home. God showed me a way that I could reach out to this child. A month later I wrote another card for a child who, frankly, had been getting on my nerves. Again, God gave me insight to understand this child's feelings and showed me what I could do to reach him. By Christmas he gave his life to the Lord. In fact, he is now an effective leader in our church and has a teaching ministry for troubled boys.

"God was leading me in this exciting journey called *prayer!* After the other teacher and I shared what God was teaching us, other teachers began to pray in the same way. Our department came to be known as a 'powerhouse of prayer.' The impact began to ripple out and led to a prayer revival that transformed our church."

I love when I hear stories like this one! I remember an experience of my own that had a life-changing impact. I had been praying for one particular child for a long time. You know the kind—you love him in the Lord, but you're not sure you like him so much? Well, on one very busy Missions Sunday, Sam came to class early, while I was still setting things up for the lesson. He began taking everything down about as fast as I could put it up.

Before I could express my exasperation, I remembered my earlier prayer for him. At that time, the Lord had put into my mind the symbol for a fish. I had assumed the fish represented a Christian, and I thought the Lord was saying to 'get this kid into the kingdom'—which is what I had been earnestly praying for! But to make conversation, I asked him, "Sam, do you like fish?"

"Yuck, I hate fish," he said. "But I do like to fish!"

"Who do you go fishing with?" I asked.

His face dropped and he replied sadly, "Nobody since my daddy left."

When I asked him if he would like for me to find someone to take him fishing, he was ecstatic. That week I found an older gentleman in our church who loved to fish. The two became fishing buddies, and it was the older man who led Sam to the Lord. God *does* answer prayer, I learned—it just may not be in the way we think he will.

There is power in prayer! The key is simply to begin with the first step. God will do the rest. Praying for that student who may annoy you will allow the Lord an opportunity to bond the two of you in Christian love.

When we depend on people, we see what people will do.
When we pray and depend on God, we see what God will do.

In my own life, I have found that during times of major crises, I have often experienced the most peace. I attribute this to the power of prayer. I have learned from painful experience not to leave for a speaking trip unless I know that several people are praying for me. Without their prayer, I'm likely to find that my luggage gets lost or my slides fall out of projector or I get sick. I can tell when others are praying for me by a special presence that cannot be explained apart from prayer.

Prayer Modeled by the Master

Just as Jesus is our model for teaching, he is our model for prayer. We can learn a great deal about how to pray by studying his prayer recorded in John 17. The progression he used in that prayer is interesting. First, he prayed for himself—that he might bring honor and glory to the Father. Second, he prayed for those closest to him, his disciples. Finally, he prayed for all believers.

We can apply the same progression to our prayers as teachers. We can pray first for ourselves—that God would be honored and glorified in our lives and specifically in our teaching. Using the letter "p" to help remind us, we can pray that God would

- be honored by our *praise*
- *purify* our motives
- *prepare* us to seek his face and to do his will
- help us *persist,* even when we don't feel like it
- *personalize* his Word to our hearts
- help us trust his *provision*

Next, we can pray for those closest to us in the classroom: our students. We can

- thank God for the *privilege* of being part of their lives
- *petition* for their needs
- ask God to *prepare* their *paths* for service

Finally, we can pray for those whose lives are indirectly touched by our teaching ministry:

- *parents* and families of our students
- *peers* whose lives the children will impact
- *pastors* and our greater church ministry

Jesus gave us another model prayer in Matthew 6:9-13. He told us where to pray in Matthew 6:6. He also said, "If you abide in me, and my words abide in you, ask whatever you wish, and it will be done for you" (John 15:7).

The Bible says much about prayer. Take time to look up some of the following passages and select one that specifically ministers to you. Commit it to memory. Process it with God as you pray. Ponder it as you go about your daily activities. See what God will teach you as you "dwell richly" on the passage (Colossians 3:16).

- "Ask and it will be given to you; seek and you will find; knock and the door will be opened to you. For everyone who asks receives; he who seeks finds; and to him who knocks, the door will be opened" (Matthew 7:7-8).
- "This is the confidence we have in approaching God: that if we ask anything according to his will, he hears us. And if we know that he hears us—whatever we ask—we know that we have what we asked of him" (1 John 5:14-15).

• "Then you will call upon me and come and pray to me, and I will listen to you" (Jeremiah 29:12).

• "I tell you the truth, my Father will give you whatever you ask in my name. Until now you have not asked for anything in my name. Ask and you will receive, and your joy will be complete" (John 16:23-24).

• "And I will do whatever you ask in my name, so that the Son may bring glory to the Father. You may ask me for anything in my name, and I will do it" (John 14:13-14).

• "But when you pray, go into your room, close the door and pray to your Father, who is unseen. Then your Father, who sees what is done in secret, will reward you" (Matthew 6:6).

Don't stop with these examples! You will be blessed as you discover even more Scriptures that lead you into a deeper reliance on God through prayer.

Roadblocks to Prayer

Paul said in Romans 7:15, "For that which I am doing, I do not understand; for I am not practicing what I would like to do, but I am doing the very thing I hate" (New American Standard). These are words to which most of us can relate. We want to be praying effectively for our students, but something stops us. What prevents us from being more effective? Let's look at some of the roadblocks that keep us from developing a fruitful prayer ministry.

1. Satan

We are commanded to "Put on the full armor of God so that you can take your stand against the devil's schemes. For our struggle is not against flesh and blood, but against the rulers, against the authorities, against the powers of this dark world and against the spiritual forces of evil in the heavenly realms" (Ephesians 6:11-12). Even Jesus had to get Satan to leave him alone. How did he do it? He quoted Scripture to him! We need to be ready with a verse to speak out loud the next time we feel Satan trying to stop us from having a powerful prayer ministry.

2. Sin

Sometimes we have unconfessed sin in our lives that prevents us from having an effective prayer life. We need to ask the Holy Spirit to reveal sin to us that we are unaware of. "If we confess our sins, he is faithful and just and will forgive us our sins and purify us from all unrighteousness" (1 John 1:9).

3. Selfishness

Selfish motives rob us of the power of prayer. We need to search our hearts in the presence of God. What is our purpose in praying for something? "When you ask, you do not receive, because you ask with wrong motives, that you may spend what you get on your pleasures" (James 4:3).

4. Self-esteem issues

Sometimes we think God will never answer our prayers because we are too "unworthy." God does call us to have humble spirits, but he also wants us to come to him as little children, believing. "Let us then approach the throne of grace with confidence, so that we may receive mercy and find grace to help us in our time of need" (Hebrews 4:16).

5. A spirit of unforgiveness

A bitter or unforgiving spirit may keep us from receiving the blessing of forgiveness ourselves. "And when you stand praying, if you hold anything against anyone, forgive him, so that your Father in heaven may forgive you your sins" (Mark 11:25).

Practical Steps to Prayer

Just as there are roadblocks that keep us from a more effective prayer life, there are steps that can help us overcome these obstacles and attain a life of consistently powerful prayer.

The Priority of Prayer

The first step is to make prayer a priority. There is wisdom in putting prayer first in our day because we all know "later" rarely comes. Daily life has a way of filling the hours and consuming precious moments we could have spent with the Lord. Use your understanding of your own personality and learning style to help you determine when you can most effectively meet with God in prayer. Write it into your schedule if necessary, and make a covenant with a friend to keep you accountable.

God is patient. He will wait when other people or things clamor for our attention. But we will bear the consequences within ourselves. I'm reminded of a number of old adages that tell us this in different ways:

- "Seven days without prayer makes one weak."
- "Life is fragile; handle with prayer."
- "A day hemmed in prayer seldom unravels."

I often think about how my prayer life parallels my other great love relationship: my marriage. My husband and I will go several days at a time carrying on only surface-level conversations about the mundane necessities and activities of life. Sometimes, given our hectic schedules, we are glad to get that much talking in! We don't let those conversations *hinder* our relationship. In fact, we find mundane communication about who will taxi which child to what event quite necessary. But we don't really build our relationship on them, either.

In the same way, many of my conversations with God are rather mundane, and carried on sort of "in passing": "God, please help me know what to say to my son"; "Lord, please give your healing touch to my neighbor who had an accident, and show me what I can do for her"; "Thank you, Father, for the glorious way the sun reflects off the mountains this afternoon." And God responds to those short prayers. He gives me wisdom to handle family hassles. He nudges me to call my neighbor. I sense his delight when I honor his handiwork. These exchanges are as much a part of my life as breathing. But they are not the stuff that deepens my relationship with God.

Engaging in prayer serves much the same purpose as a dinner date. It is a time when I set aside everything else for the express purpose of *knowing* God. If I pass up opportunities to sit and really converse with my husband, giving him my undivided attention, I find that our daily, more mundane interchanges lose some of their efficiency. When I don't understand where he's coming from, I find myself easily irritated or sometimes just plain confused.

In the same way, when I bypass real prayer time, I find myself feeling interrupted by the prompting of the Holy Spirit or confused by some of his nudges. Eventually, those feelings hinder my relationship with God. I become less effective in ministry. I am confident that God in his sovereignty goes on to accomplish his purpose with or without me, but I lose the blessing of serving him.

Praise God that this is not an irreconcilable difference! When I am faithless, he remains faithful (2 Timothy 2:13) and sets our relationship right as I am obedient in prayer.

Nothing you can do to make yourself a treasured teacher will ever substitute for the power that comes from your relationship with God. Ask God for a

Christlike character rather than just temporal answers to needs. Circumstances change, but character is developed in the practice of prayer as a priority.

Prayer Prompts

As another step to powerful prayer, make use of "prayer prompts." What's a prayer prompt? It is any tool we can use to remind us and assist us to be faithful in prayer. Here are some prompts I recommend:

• Keep a stash of 3x5 note cards in a box in the classroom, and give your students some time during the hour in which they can write down their prayer requests. I do this, and I find that these written requests are often different from the requests shared out loud during our class prayer time. I keep the cards private and pray over the requests during the week.

As the year progresses, the children open up more, and my praying for their requests strengthens the bond between us. It's as if the Lord builds bridges between our souls through this time of prayer. Sometimes the look in their eyes or something they share lets me know that they know I am praying for them. Together, we share the joy of answered prayer. We grow as we learn that sometimes God answers "no." All in all, our spiritual journey together is deepened.

• Write response cards back to the students to tell them when you prayed for their requests. Your accountability to a child can be a powerful motivator. You may want to start this project on a small scale so that you never disappoint one of your kids.

• Write notes to yourself relating to your learners' comments or prayer requests. Perhaps something that is said will prompt you to pray for a certain behavior change. For example: "I pray for Johnny to be more patient with his peers," or "I pray for Katie to be more helpful in her home."

• Simply pray down your class roster. You could pray for one child per week and go down the list in that way, or you may pray for a certain number of students each day of the week.

• Pray intensively for students during their birthday months.

• Pray in "concentric circles" around each child. (See the sample on p. 81.) Or simply imagine the children's relationship with Christ as the center of a circle. Around them are parents, then school relationships, then future relationships, then their impact on the world at large. Pray for them in each of these arenas.

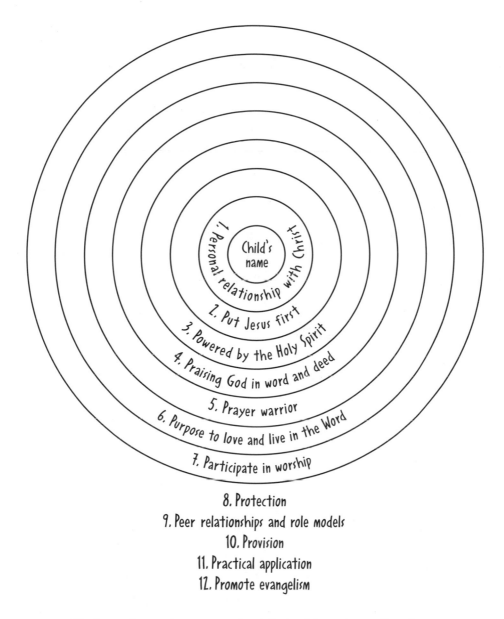

Child's name

1. Personal relationship with Christ
2. Put Jesus first
3. Powered by the Holy Spirit
4. Praising God in word and deed
5. Prayer warrior
6. Purpose to love and live in the Word
7. Participate in worship

8. Protection
9. Peer relationships and role models
10. Provision
11. Practical application
12. Promote evangelism

• Photograph your learners, and put their pictures in a gallery frame near your prayer area. Somehow, when you look into the eyes of a child, you get all kinds of inspiration for how to pray!

• Choose a verse to pray for each student. Write each child's name on a ribbon, and use the ribbons to mark passages. Here are some suggested Scriptures to get you started:

"And this is my prayer for [child's name]: that [his or her] love may abound more and more in knowledge and depth of insight" (from Philippians 1:9).

"Dear Lord, instruct [child's name] and teach [him or her] in the way [he or she] should go; counsel [child's name] and watch over [him or her]" (from Psalm 32:8).

"Jesus, help [child's name] to be strengthened with all power according to his glorious might so that [he or she] may have great endurance and patience, and joyfully give thanks to the Father..." (from Colossians 1:11-12).

• Highlight areas of special concern that you have for each child. Don't get overburdened trying to pray in all categories for each child every day. You don't have time, and you'll get discouraged. Remember, the purpose is to build an effective intercessory prayer life for your students—not to create more work for you. View prayer as a ministry, and the Lord will help you to carry the load.

Praying With Our Students

The most effective way to teach prayer is to model prayer. I remember a particular Wednesday night in January 1991. People were just arriving for midweek church activities when the commencement of Desert Storm, the battle in the Middle East, was announced. Our thoughts turned immediately to prayer. In each classroom, we read to the children from Ephesians 6, assuring them that our battle is not against flesh and blood but against the devil's schemes, and reminding them of the full armor God provides. Then we prayed together. That night, prayer was like a big security blanket that we wrapped around each child.

In times of stress and confusion, prayer is so important! Our prayer that night modeled for our students what to do in such circumstances: Go to our Heavenly Father and talk to him.

Prayer should be a part of each hour in our church programs. Again, children learn more from our attitudes about prayer and our modeling of prayer than from what we tell them about prayer. If we are excited to pray, that excitement will be contagious to our students. If we are consistent in prayer time, we will train our students in the habit of prayer.

Practical Prayer Projects

Several ways to train students in prayer habits are found in chapter 7 of my book *Cherishing and Challenging Your Children.* For information about obtaining a copy, call (972) 239-3850, fax (972) 239-2968, or e-mail me at jcapehart@ bigplanet.com. More ideas can be gleaned from *Hooray! Let's Pray!* (Group Publishing, Inc., 1997). Here are several things you can do right away.

For preschoolers:

• *Folding hands.* Invite the kids to imitate your hand motions. Then wiggle your thumbs and say, "Prayer is talking to Jesus. What do you want to tell *Jesus?* We can thank him, praise him, or tell him something."

Wiggle the three middle fingers. Say: "Our next three fingers remind us to pray for others. Who do we want to pray for? our family? our friends? our missionaries? our teachers? those who are sick? those in our church? Let's pray for *others.*"

Wiggle your little finger and say, "As we wiggle our little finger, we think of ourselves. What do you want to pray for? What do you want to tell Jesus that *you* need?" Then fold your hands together and pray.

This process trains preschoolers to put *Jesus* first, *others* next and *"you"* last. The first letters of those three words, of course, spell "joy."

• *Classroom prayers.* Have children each pick up something in the classroom they are thankful for (a toy or a picture, perhaps). Gather in your prayer area. Begin by offering a simple open-ended prayer, such as: "God, you have given us many things to be thankful for. These are a few things from our classroom that we really like…" Then let preschoolers each name the item they have selected. Close by saying "amen" together.

• *Picture book prayers.* Many board books have simple, one-page pictures. (Animal books are especially appropriate.) Open the pages one at a time, and have the children say, "Thank God for…," naming the object or item in the picture.

• *Action prayers.* Try one of these active rhymes to direct your preschoolers' attention to God:

For story time:

I can jump! *(Children jump.)*

I can turn! *(Children turn in circle.)*

Help me listen so I can learn! *(Children sit down.)*
Amen!

Before leaving:
Thank you for your Holy Word. *(Hold hands open like a book.)*
Thank you for my class. *(Children pat each other's backs.)*
Help me remember what I learned *(touch temple)*
And run to do what you ask. *(Run in place.)*
Aaaaaaa- *(children continue running)* men!" *(Children stop abruptly.)*

For elementary-age children:

• *Prayer partners.* Children come to an age when they may not be comfortable sharing personal prayer requests with the entire class. This may be the time to introduce the idea of prayer partners. Pair each student with a classmate that you feel will be a compatible prayer partner. Allow time in each class session for them to pray together.

Stress that this is a time of prayer and not gossip or play. It is very important to train our students in the wisdom of not repeating a person's prayer requests as gossip. Nothing will hurt students more and compromise their ability to be vulnerable in prayer than to have their confidence breached.

Consider a fourth-grade boy who has been carrying the long-time burden of having an alcoholic parent. In disclosing this personal secret and the pain of the situation, he is blessed to know that someone is praying. However, if word that "Johnny's father drinks" becomes gossip fodder for the church and eventually reaches that parent, Johnny is in trouble. A vulnerability shared in an atmosphere of trust now becomes a liability. How sad. How unnecessary. Please, let's respect each other's right to privacy, and teach our kids to do the same!

• *Prayer countdown.* When preparing to pray with a large group of children, I like to give everyone a limited time period to settle down and shift their focus to prayer. Calling out a "Countdown to Prayer" works quite well: "Ten, nine, eight, seven, six, five, four, three, two, one, *bow!*" The kids know I expect absolute silence at that moment.

• *Prayer walk.* Take your students to different locations, stopping for silent prayer at each place. Try walking around the church property to pray for the needs of the congregation or outdoors in the neighborhood to pray about evangelism opportunities.

- *Prayer time line.* Post a time line that covers the duration of your class year. Let kids each post a prayer request on the day they bring the request up, and post notes along the time line as they see God answering the prayer.

- *Draw a prayer.* List prayer requests on index cards. Hold all the cards in your hand, upside down, and let each child draw out one of the cards. Have the children gather in a circle. Go around the circle in order, and let the children each either verbalize the prayer or carry the card to the center of the circle to signify they have chosen to pray silently for the need.

- *Forgiveness prayers.* Let children practice confession by allowing them each time to write their sin on a piece of paper. Let them close their eyes and signify when they are through praying by wadding up the paper and carrying it to the wastepaper basket.

Since prayer is a privilege, I tell students the reason we close our eyes and fold our hands for prayer is to focus our complete attention on God. If we're looking around or fidgeting with something, we are less likely to be focused on the Lord. Does God only answer the prayers of children who sit quietly and close their eyes and fold their hands? Of course not! God answers the prayers we pray from our hearts—but quiet hands can help our hearts to be more quiet.

Let your own enthusiasm and a hands-on perspective direct your prayer times with children. Don't be afraid to allow kids creative expression during prayer. Remember, Jacob wrestled as he spoke with the angel of the Lord; David sang out his requests; Peter had a great vision that communicated God's message as he slept; and Paul wrote out his prayers in letters. What great models of the rich expressiveness of man to God, and God to man!

Inner Direction

As you think about these questions, make a note of related personal experiences or Scriptures that contribute to your understanding.

1. When have you found prayer most important in your life?

_____

_____

2. What distracts you from prayer?

_____

_____

3. Think of a time when someone prayed for you. How did you feel about that prayer support?

_____

_____

4. When have you effectively prayed with a child? What do you think facilitated that effectiveness?

_____

_____

5. Select a way to pray for one or more of your students this week. Pray for a month, and share the results with a partner.

_____

_____

ENDNOTES

1. Richard Foster, *Celebration of Discipline* (San Francisco, CA: Harper and Row, 1988), 33.
2. Edward McKendree Bounds, *Power Through Prayer* (Ada, MI: Baker Book House, 1992), 23.
3. Pennsylvania Online. "Streams of Light," January 18, 1997. Go to http://www.paonline.com/streams and click on "Archives."

Chapter 6
The Need for Nurturing

Treasured teachers see the need to nurture students and find appropriate ways to demonstrate love, encouragement, and support.

"The giant oak sleeps in the acorn…Grandma's apple pie rests
patiently in the appleseed…and within every young soul
is a great vision for life, awaiting nurture…"
—Joe White,
What Kids Wish Parents Knew About Parenting

"Beloved, let us love one another, for love is from God;
and everyone who loves is born of God and knows God"
(1 John 4:7, New American Standard)

It started out as a normal day. The two-year-old boy had said goodbye to his father, who was headed to the office, at about 8:00 that morning. The boy and his mother were home alone, as they were most days at that time. But half an hour later, the mother had a massive heart attack and died. The traumatized child was alone all day with his dead mother until his father returned at 6:00 that evening.

When the child reached second grade, his father and new stepmother sought out the school where I was principal because they had heard it was very nurturing and loving. They felt our environment was just what he needed in a school experience in order to heal. I agonized for this child and realized the situation would be difficult. We prayed about it; I felt the Lord saying "yes," and we took the child.

He was a major challenge. Sometimes for no apparent reason he would begin to scream or cry. Many days I carried him down the hall as he screamed, and I rocked him for hours in my office. The classroom teacher met with him each day before class and prayed with him. She was a tremendous nurturer and did much to facilitate his healing.

One day after chapel, I found him sobbing in a fetal position. I stayed with him as he cried, "I feel love…I feel love…I feel Jesus loving me…" He accepted Christ that day. Yes, love does heal!

I strongly believe that children have an intense need to be touched and nurtured. Without love, our teaching remains on the pedagogical periphery and does not impact or mold our students internally where true learning takes place. Our words remain hollow if we do not bond them to our students with our love.

There is a great need for nurturing today. Children often come to Sunday school from difficult home situations. According to widely accepted statistics, about half of our children come from broken homes, and an even higher percentage come from dysfunctional families. The children we teach are often hurting, bewildered, and angry.

As treasured teachers, we can be like an oasis of love for them. They can cling to us in the raging storms of life, and we can bring them to the stability and peace Jesus Christ offers. We can do much to keep them from going adrift in a world that often doesn't care. The need for nurturing teachers who truly love their students abounds.

As a principal, I looked carefully for the degree of nurturing in a person I might hire as a teacher. I preferred to have a loving, nurturing teacher with one degree in teaching than a highly trained teacher with many degrees who could not nurture children. We experienced the fruit of this decision as parents came to observe our operation. Their consistent feedback was, "This is a very loving school."

I am a self-proclaimed "rocking chair therapist." To me, a rocking chair exemplifies nurturing. Placing one in a classroom is like setting up a neon sign that flashes, "I love my students."

Back in the seventies, before I had my own children, I observed the trend of more mothers taking jobs outside the home. Concerned about the lack of nurturing their kids would experience, I designed a day-care facility with a room in the middle that was a "nurturing center." It had wide open, bright areas; a cozy corner with pillows; lots of baskets of books; and rocking chairs all over. This was the "Rocking Womb." I wanted moms to come to the center any time they could get away from their offices and nurse, nurture, and be with their children. I also designed a lunchroom where moms and dads could eat with their kids. At the time I was excited because I saw the center as a "win-win" for children and their parents. Several corporations heard about my plan and gave me well-padded budgets to develop nurturing centers for their employees.

Something was wrong, however. Finally I realized that if I continued to provide this warm, loving, nurturing environment, I would make it too easy for some mothers to work outside the home. I wrestled for a long time with this conviction. My heart ached for the children whose moms *had* to work. I wanted to nurture them with everything I had in me. In fact, I often invited kids to come home with me to spend the night. I knew how much they needed that extra bit of nurturing. Just as a flower opens up when given proper sun, water, and soil, so does a child when given attention, a gentle touch, encouragement, and a nurturing environment.

After much soul-searching, I decided to stop providing these centers. I began to pray for more moms to find ways to be home with their children. I also began to encourage nurturing friends to offer in-home child care for moms who had to work.

Appropriate Nurturing

We must be sensitive about how we nurture. For example, what is appropriate touch? Is it the same when kids are two as when they are ten?

I believe very little children should be held, hugged, and rocked. In the elementary years, a hug remains appropriate for many of them. As they begin to develop physically, a sideways hug becomes more suitable. Later, as children become self-conscious about hugs, I find that just a pat on the shoulder as I pass their desk or chair is enough.

Older children who are uncomfortable about outwardly expressing their care find more subtle ways to touch: standing especially close as they ask a question, for example. Since I'm a "toucher," I often let older children sit or stand close. I still hug, pat, touch, and squeeze a shoulder. Parents often tell me that their child seeks me out to get "their hug"!

We all need love; we just become more sophisticated in how we express it as we grow up. If children receive enough positive and appropriate nurturing at home and in teaching situations, they won't be as vulnerable to inappropriate physical outlets that will hurt them and get them in trouble.

Being a visually oriented person, I love pictures. One of my favorites is a print of Jesus cupping the face of a child and tenderly looking into the child's eyes. Other children are close by, and the nurturing in his touch is unmistakable. I believe that is how Jesus would be around children. Treasured teachers seeking to be like Jesus need to nurture their students with the same tender yet tough love. John, known as "the apostle of love," writes in John 13:1, "Having loved his own who were in the world, he loved them to the end" (NAS).

There are different levels of nurturing, and Jesus incorporated them all. Physically, he touched people. He held children. He healed. Emotionally, he encouraged and supported. He had no hidden agendas or codependent motives; he simply loved people! Intellectually, he connected to their own life experiences to teach profound, life-changing lessons. Spiritually, he gave the ultimate gift of nurturing as he laid down his life. He was the ultimate Good Shepherd.

Each of us has our own "language of nurturing"—the words and behaviors we use to express love and care. We need to think about and be aware of the ways that work best for us. Which of the following do you use?

Physically nurturing behaviors
- Making eye contact
- Being close
- Giving hugs
- Giving pats on the shoulder or back
- Rocking

Emotionally nurturing behaviors
- Praising
- Affirming
- Encouraging
- Investing time

Intellectually nurturing behaviors
- Sharing something you've researched because it interests a student
- Reading a book of special interest together
- Nurturing and encouraging a child's best efforts

Spiritually nurturing behaviors
- Sharing God's love with students by actions, not just words

- Praying with a child
- Highlighting a child's spiritual insights

Nurturing as Part of the Teaching Process

Why is nurturing important in the process of teaching in the church? In *Education That Is Christian* we read:

"The focus in teaching is for the pupil to hear God speak a personal word to him and for him to respond personally. The Lord always takes the initiative, in love revealing himself and his will. We teachers work with him to get the pupil ready to listen in the context of his or her daily life, which is the only situation that has meaning for him or her. Revelation demands response. God says, 'I have made all this provision for you; I expect this of you in return.' He wants to set up personal relationships with each pupil, ever more intimate. Christianity is person-to-person."[1]

Educators now know that stress, feelings of fear, and threats of harm impair the brain's ability to learn. May children never experience such things in our classrooms! On the opposite side, children who experience warm and nurturing learning situations are motivated to learn through positive relationships. They are able to learn from their mistakes and develop a sense of competence that allows them to excel. If those things are important in developing academic and emotional maturity, consider how much more important they are for developing spiritual maturity!

The ABCs of Nurturing

Nurturing our students is as easy as A-B-C:

A—Accept all your learners as God made them. Each is a unique part of their classroom, church, and the kingdom.

B—Believe in your students. Many children have no one that simply believes in them. Church may be the only place where some kids find adults who think they are winners.

C—Celebrate birthdays and other special events. There are many ways to do this. The very fact that you know and acknowledge your students' landmarks is a celebration in itself!

D—Develop relationships. Step outside the classroom door! If a student needs some special relationship-building time, you may want to prayerfully consider a home visit—or just taking the child out for ice cream. I have found that simply asking a child to accompany me on an errand builds a relationship. Research from the Search Institute tells us that children need support from three or more nonparent adults to grow up healthy, competent, and caring.[2]

E—Encourage effort. Look for more than the final outcome of your students' attempts. Encourage them in the process of trying!

F—Find something to praise each child for each Sunday. When I mentioned this at a teacher's convention, someone responded, "The only positive thing I can say about one of my students is, 'I sure am glad you don't go home with me!' " We laugh at this, but we have all experienced the same feeling about a child at some time. Pray about it, and don't let yourself off the hook!

G—Give tokens of affection kids don't have to earn. Kids love little touchable or tastable reminders of your affirmation. When my children were very little, a dear man used to stand at the door of the sanctuary and give each child a piece of hard candy from his pocket. He didn't withhold the candy from a child who wiggled or didn't sing. He just let each one know he was glad they were there. Years later, my kids still remember that Mr. Jim liked them and made them feel happy to be at church.

H—Have plenty of "certificates" on hand. Carry some index cards and a package of stickers with you. When kids do something for which you have been praying, show progress in an area, or simply need to know that you care, jot them a quick note and hand it to them as they leave that day.

I—Initiate conversations. Call students on the phone, stop them in the hallway, or most importantly, ask for their input when you are talking to another adult in their presence. (Check in with the parents before you ask to speak with a child on the phone.)

J—Just say no. Provide firm and consistent limits to help children feel secure.

K—Kindly present the truth. Children need our honest feedback. Let children know when they are not meeting your expectations in a firm but kind manner.

L—Listen and laugh. Take the time to really attend to what a child has to say. Handle difficult situations with humor, and be careful to always laugh *with* kids—never *at* them.

M—Make your class a safe place. Banish put-down humor and sarcasm. Never let a child be the brunt of anyone else's bad attitude.

N—Never underestimate your students' potential. Remember, God has often used children to accomplish his purposes!

O—Offer yourself as a champion. Commit to being the person who always hopes, always perseveres, always looks to the best interests of each of your students.

P—Point to God's plans. Affirm that God has a plan for the life of each of your students. They need to know that the God of the universe has a design for their lives.

Q—Question children in ways that make them think. Even little ones don't always need the easy answers. They will learn much more if you help them develop their own conclusions through effective questioning.

R—Respect children's boundaries. Don't make every issue a challenge to your authority. If a child is truly too tired, hungry, scared, or shy to do what you've asked, offer a respectful alternative that will work for both of you.

S—Stay on top of what's going on in a child's life. We live in a busy society and home visits may no longer be common, but they can be one of the most powerful ways of enhancing your ministry. You can quickly get a window into your students' lives when you visit them at home.

T—Treasure the child. Take every opportunity to tell children how precious they are to God and to you. There are many thousands of ways to say how much you love a child. A love song I learned long ago to sing to my own children says it best: "I'm blessed to have you as part of my life."

U—Understand before assessing. Try to understand what is motivating a child before judging harshly. No child's behavior occurs in a vacuum.

V—Value children in the same way Jesus did. Remember that the kingdom of heaven belongs not to the rich and famous but to "such as these."

W—Wait. We live in the era of "hurry up." Many of our frustrations could be eliminated if we just waited! Wait for a child to process your request; wait until that one last cotton ball is on the paper; wait until a child thinks of an answer; wait until "that phase" is over.

X—Exchange one of your plans for one of theirs. Sometimes flexibility can save the day!

Y—Yell only in encouragement. Save the shouts for baseball games and swim meets. Speak with a respectfully modulated voice during class.

Z—Zip your lips to criticism. Address problems as they arise. Never fall into the trap of criticizing children in or out of their presence.

As you can see through these ABCs, the overwhelming message to our children needs to be "I'm on your side." Unconditional love and nurturing does not mean automatic approval for every choice students make. Quite the contrary—we want to encourage behavior that is consistent with our best beliefs about who the children are and who they can become in Christ.

Nurturing Special Children

Under the canopy of nurturing, I want to address the subject of teaching children with special needs. I am well aware that I may violate some people's comfort zones in discussing this, but I feel strongly about the issue. By closing the door to my involvement in a home/school ministry to children with multiple handicaps early in my career, God led me on a lifelong quest to incorporate some of these special children into the "normal" education system.

Ministry to some disabled children and their families is a difficult challenge. Many people are uncomfortable with disabilities in general. But in my experience, the effort is far outweighed by the reward.

When I watch an autistic child say "Jesus" and reach out to a teacher, I know it's worth it. When I see a couple of "rough-and-tumble" boys comfort a child with cerebral palsy through a seizure and help him change his clothes, I know it's worth it. When I see children brainstorm solutions to accommodate a friend's wheelchair, I know that God is bringing a special sensitivity into their lives they might not otherwise have developed.

Yes, there are days when the autistic child is loud and disruptive, the visually impaired child needs extra assistance, or the wheelchair-bound student has an embarrassing accident. But these children also have incredible gifts to offer. If we plan to teach our students about the breadth of God's love, kindness, and compassion and the value of each individual to his heart, we had better live it! The more we expose children to people with a variety of needs, the more understanding and compassionate they will become. They will learn to not pull back out of fear of the unknown but to embrace the differences. After all, isn't that Christianity in action?

I love and respect Joni Eareckson Tada tremendously. She has learned to live beyond the handicap that could have sidelined her for life. Her ministry, Joni and Friends, has adopted a ministry vision statement I'd like to share with you:

JAF Ministries Vision

We envision a world in which:

• The gospel is communicated to every person with a disability, giving them the opportunity to respond to the claims of Christ.

• The church values people with disabilities, and finds ways for them to use their gifts.

• Families with a disabled member are strengthened through a community of Christian support, experiencing stability and capacity to remain faithful to one another.

• Christians pray for people with disabilities and are personally involved in disability ministry.

• Pastors and missionaries present God's perspective regarding suffering from the pulpit as a part of their ministry vision.

• Churches around the world are transformed into a positive influence that is accessible, responsive, and committed to the evangelistic and discipleship needs in the disability community. [3]

I believe this vision for ministry should permeate all aspects of our church programs. Does this mean that we have to establish specialized ministries? Not necessarily. An attitude of love and acceptance will draw all kinds of families to your church. Each time I've encountered a different kind of disability, I've been stretched as I've learned how to work with and support the family.

Sometimes that learning has required special course work. Other times, I've needed to be taught how to do specific medical procedures "just in case." At yet other times, I've had to walk hand-in-hand with a family through "the valley of the shadow of death." It has not been easy. But I can testify that it has been the very act of stretching that has strengthened and enriched my life. I'm thankful for the special children God has allowed me to minister to.

We not only need to be open to special children, but to special teachers as well. My brother-in-law, Dennis Dordigan, contracted multiple sclerosis during his last year at Dallas Theological Seminary and is now confined to a wheelchair. He was a powerful preacher when he was in prime physical condition, but he is even more powerful now—even though his voice quavers and his wife has to look up the Bible passages for him. He could be a bitter, disillusioned, broken man. But when you see him, hear him teach, listen to one of the joyful songs he's composed, or witness one of the many monologues that he has written and dramatized, you see the Lord Jesus.

Dennis exemplifies true joy in the midst of suffering. When I am having a pity party over my minor afflictions, I am reminded of Dennis, and I am humbled. Dennis is a treasured teacher. It is from people with testimonies like his that I want children to learn.

Inner Direction

As you think about these questions, make a note of related personal experiences or Scriptures that contribute to your understanding.

1. What do you believe about children's needs for nurturing?

_____

_____

2. List ways that you can nurture children more effectively on the physical, emotional, intellectual, and spiritual levels.

_____

_____

3. What are some ABCs of nurture you would add?

_____

_____

4. What do you believe about children with special needs?

_____

_____

5. What goals do you have for your church regarding people with disabilities?

_____

_____

ENDNOTES

1. Lois E. Lebar and James E. Plueddemann, *Education That Is Christian* (Wheaton, IL: Victor Books, 1989), 150.
2. Search Institute, "Forty Developmental Assets." Available at http://www.search-institute.org/assets
3. JAF, "JAF Ministries Vision." Go to http://www.jafministries.com/about/annual and click on twelve.html.

Chapter 7
Caring Communication

Treasured teachers are caring communicators who provide the right learning climate to help children grow in character, content, and conduct.

In order to communicate God, we need to get close to people,
understand their needs, fears, hopes and dreams, and then
start at that point and preach Jesus to them, putting the
story into words and illustrations they can understand.
—Leighton Ford, from *Speaker's Sourcebook*

"The tongue has the power of life and death, and
those who love it will eat its fruit" (Proverbs 18:21).

O nce on a field trip I heard a group of children discussing where they were born. "Jay was born in Miami," Samantha announced. To which Jamie responded, "Come on, was Jay really born in 'her ami'?"

This story illustrates with delightful humor the communication chaos sometimes created with language. Communication skills are essential for treasured teachers; children frequently do not have a complete grasp of the language, and many words are confusing to them. Because they are such multisensory learners, they are often "hearing" us on many levels.

Let's examine some of the basic principles of communicating with our learners.

Clearing the Channel

As teachers, we have the opportunity to communicate with our students on a variety of subjects in a variety of ways. The first law of medicine, it has been said, is "First do no harm." We would be wise to adopt this as a strategy for communicating with our learners. We want every encounter with a learner to speak of God's love, for without that we are no more than a "clanging cymbal" (1 Corinthians 13:1). Love is the glue that bonds us (and our teaching) to our students. His love gives us grace to love children even when tough situations leave us feeling anything but loving.

We need to ask ourselves, "What would Jesus say?" Sometimes the wisest thing to say is nothing at all until we feel the Lord's leading. Many times I have prayed to "put a muzzle on my mouth" (Psalm 39:1) until l felt the Lord leading me to speak. I have learned that my mouth will often get me into trouble! Jesus made every word count in his teaching. He spoke with wisdom, clarity, and love. We need to make sure that we follow his leading in all our communication.

A Christian is…
A mind
Through which Christ *thinks*
A voice
Through which Christ *speaks*
A heart
Through which Christ *loves*
A hand
Through which Christ *helps*. [1]

I challenge you to put your teaching on a tape recorder or have someone listen to you teach in class and give an honest appraisal of your communication. We are often unaware of simple things that muddy our ability to be effective communicators. For example, at one point I worked hard to eliminate the "you knows" from my speaking. A year later, as I listened to a tape of myself, I was amazed at all the "you knows" that had slipped in despite my efforts.

Of course, this wasn't a major communication flaw—simply an annoying one. But if harmless flaws can creep in, it is safe to assume that more destructive ones can as well. We all have sloppy verbiage in our memory banks that we are not aware of. Sometimes these words come out unconsciously or when we're under pressure.

An important thing to notice is how much our tone of voice impacts our message. We may find that we take a tone with students that we'd never use to address adults. That's fine if we're teaching in the early childhood department, where many of us slip into what psychologists term "mother-ese." This language—most often used by mothers with their young children—is an effective tool for teaching language and communicating nurture to the little guys. But if we are using it when we teach fifth graders, we are sure to alienate our students.

Teachers are a walking "show and tell," and children are born mimics. They observe and emulate what they see modeled for them. If we are using a demanding tone of voice, chances are that our students will mimic that. I have seen repeatedly that gentle, quiet teachers tend to have students who speak more softly in the classroom. Children often live up or down to our expectations of them.

Furthermore, because children think in concrete terms, we must be careful not to use words that conjure up images we don't want to communicate. Once, while discussing with a class how we are to give our hearts to God for his service, a teacher asked the children what they would like to give to God.

"A knife," one child promptly responded.

Knowing this child to be a deep thinker, the teacher asked, "Why a knife?"

"So he can cut a hole through the clouds to see me better" was the response. Never underestimate the power of a child's logic!

Many words in our English language can be confusing, especially to the concrete thinking of a child. Have you ever noticed that when you sing "Our God reigns..." every child in the room looks out the window to see if God is really "raining" or not? Once we sang a song in chapel with the words, "The presence of God watches over me." Upon leaving the chapel, one little guy asked when he was going to get his "present" from God—"you know, the 'watch' we sang about." Another time, a child described Promotion Sunday as "Commotion Sunday," and most of the teachers agreed. Yes, words can be confusing!

Words can build bridges to understanding, or they can create walls that keep us from that understanding. In his book, *Teaching to Change Lives,* Dr. Howard Hendricks writes: "The word 'communication' comes from the Latin word *communis,* meaning 'common.' Before we can communicate we must establish commonness, commonality. And the greater the commonality, the greater the potential for communication." [2]

Too often, however, we fail to consider how to communicate "in common" with our students. We tend to use many figurative terms as we discuss important spiritual issues, leaving our kids behind in the dust. We need to rethink our language as a child might interpret it and talk in a way that is common to both teachers and kids.

For some children, our words don't communicate at all. A child visiting her grandparents attended church for the first time. After the service, her grandfather asked her what the sermon was about. "I don't know, Grandpa," she answered. "He didn't say." A lot of us may be talking but not saying anything!

The same can be true as we read or memorize Scripture. Most Bible translations surpass children's listening vocabularies, which are more advanced than their sight vocabularies. The most simplified full-text Bible is written at about the same reading level as a newspaper—somewhere around sixth grade. Does that mean children can't understand the Scripture? Hardly! It just means that we have to take care that children don't substitute familiar meanings for unfamiliar words. If children form these misconceptions on their own, they can come up with huge gaps on which they base further understandings, sort of like building a house upon the sand.

These misconceptions become ingrained and are difficult to shake, even when children discover evidence that contradicts their thinking. To this day, I still get a visual image of an animal parade when we sing "Lead On, O King Eternal," which I was told by one imaginative child sounded like "Lead On O Kingly Turtle"!

The Character of Our Communication

To be treasured teachers, our communication with our students needs to be

1. Clear

• Seek eye contact before you deliver any communication. If you are giving directions to the whole class, "wait 'til you see the whites of their eyes." If you are talking to an individual, look directly at the child. This is important since so much of what we communicate is nonverbal.

• Seek eye level. Some research has indicated that our brains engage in response to eye motion. If you are addressing the entire class, move around a bit so that children's eyes must follow you. (Take care not to make this movement an experience in "follow the bouncing ball," which quickly becomes distracting.) If you are speaking to a young child, bend down so you can see eye-to-eye.

• Give "I messages." Say what you are thinking or feeling rather than engaging in verbal finger-pointing, such as "you never listen," or "you're not paying attention." These kinds of messages automatically call for a child's defenses to go up before they can even hear what you are saying.

2. Positive

Children often hear what *not* to do, but we forget to tell them what *to* do. Instead of "Don't hit. Don't interrupt. Don't get off your chair," try some positive statements:

- "You may use your hands to love."
- "You may listen when someone else is talking. Raise your hand and then when I call on you, you may talk."
- "You may sit on your chair until I invite you to get up to go to the next activity."
- "I like the way you are finding more ways to show love with your hands."
- "I like the way you are trying to remember to wait to talk until I call on you."
- "I like the way you are trying to remember to sit on your chair."

Another way to be positive is to choose to recognize good behavior instead of calling out bad. For example, say, "I like the way Jenny and Seth are sitting in the circle." Watch for the dangers of calling attention to the same child too often or never calling attention to the effort of a child who struggles with the behavior that you are trying to encourage.

When you can't think of something positive to say, pray. God never lets me down when I pray silently for him to show me something good about a student. Something always happens to give me a chance to sincerely praise the child.

Two teachers can be so different in this area of communicating! One may see a particular class and talk about "how bad," "how wild," or "how tough" the children are. Another may take over that class and see each child as "precious in God's sight." Within weeks those "terrible problem children" may become more loving and gentle because a treasured teacher has cultivated the positive in each child.

3. Credible

Children have an antenna for authenticity. They can sense when adults are being "real" with them. If children believe we are genuine in what we say, they will "buy into" other things we share. Likewise, if they believe we have deceived them, they may not see any of what we are sharing as credible. Credibility always factors into the effectiveness of our communication.

Sometimes we adopt a teasing relationship with children. This can be dangerous ground, since children tend to take everything we say quite literally. Even if they have reached the age when they can think a bit more abstractly, there is always the sense that teasing is built on truth. A teacher my daughter recently had fell down this slippery slope when she teasingly said, "Oh, you can't read that!" What she meant to communicate was, "I'm always pleased and surprised by how well you read." What Erin heard was that her teacher didn't think she was a good reader, and she came to the car that day in tears. Since Erin really believed that she was a good reader, the situation became even more painful. There was a gap in her trust of this teacher. I'm happy to say they worked out the misunderstanding!

Another way we threaten our credibility with children is in the way we set up activities or demonstrations. If we stretch the truth for our own purposes, then snap it back to teach a lesson, we are wordlessly teaching that the end justifies the means. The classic example of this is the misuse of "gospel illusion" (otherwise known as magic tricks) to teach a Bible lesson. Properly used, these activities may involve withholding some key information, but they will never make the learners (especially the Thinkers) feel that they've been lied to. Good learning activities are always run through the credibility filter: Can I set this activity up without telling an untruth?

4. Consistent with learner style

In chapter 3, we spoke about using the words that best communicate with particular learner styles (p. 49). Let's get more specific in looking for lines of communication that will make the most sense to each style.

- To *Lookers,* present yourself in a way that
  Is straightforward
  Is step-by-step
  Uses gestures (like ticking off your points on your fingers)
  Emphasizes practicality
  Frequently makes use of written communication
  Demonstrates more than explains
  Appreciates their viewpoint
  Accounts for the mind pictures they will inevitably form

- To *Talkers*, present yourself in a way that

  Is conversational

  Asks for input

  Observes their state of readiness to hear

  Reassures them of the strength of your relationship

  Minimizes pressure

  Offers frequent feedback

  Seeks commonality

  Allows for response time

- To *Explorers*, present yourself in a way that

  Takes advantage of their sense of humor

  Is focused on the end result with space to explore how to get there

  Is not dogmatic

  Communicates flexibility

  Appreciates enthusiasm

  Is clear about your own limits

  Offers options

  Allows for multitasking (listening to you while doing something else)

- To *Thinkers*, present yourself in a way that

  Is well-documented

  Is linear

  Is logical rather than emotional

  Emphasizes cause-and-effect or logical consequences

  Gives reasons leading to your conclusion

  Is goal-oriented

  Is factually detailed

  Is not threatened by their search for corroborating evidence

Obviously, when you are communicating to a whole group of learners, the lines of communication you will be most comfortable with are your own (and your style may cause you to feel frustrated at the vagueness of each of these communication lines as they are presented here!). You cannot be flexible for the Explorers while at the same time giving the Lookers the detail they need to form a visual image. But these guidelines will help you immensely when you are seeking for the best way to communicate one-on-one.

5. Compassionate rather than condemning

As we communicate with children, especially at times when emotions are running high, we need to concern ourselves more with being a "mirror" than a critic. Notice how Jesus dealt with Mary when she expressed her grief and frustration about her brother's death in John 11:32-36. Jesus was touched by her raw feelings and wept with her (although he dealt with her sister, Martha, in a different way, based on her own unique personality). Jesus didn't say, "Now, there, don't cry." He acknowledged Mary's pain and reflected it back to her.

We don't have to be overtly critical to stamp the sign "condemned" on children's feelings. We unintentionally shut them down with words we intend to be comforting or peace-making, such as, "It's OK. Don't cry. It's not that big a deal." It's a very big deal to them—otherwise they wouldn't be crying!

We need to learn to communicate the same kind of acceptance Jesus offered Mary. This doesn't mean we don't expect children to handle their emotions effectively. We simply provide them with the opportunity to exercise self-control within an atmosphere of understanding. We begin to do that by learning to identify condemning and compassionate responses like these:

Condemning:	*Compassionate:*
"You shouldn't be so upset."	"I can see that made you angry. What would it take to help you forgive?"
"That's nothing to cry about."	"You're feeling really sad. I feel sad sometimes, too."
"Be good and stop crying."	"It's all right, we all need to cry sometimes."
"How could you possibly have done that?"	"What might work better next time?"

We must try to empathize with what our children are going through. Childhood can be a very challenging and traumatic time. To hear, "Oh come on, what's wrong with you? Don't you know these are the best years of your life?" may cause them not to want the rest of their lives! Before we judge a child, let us pray that we understand what living that child's life is like.

What about times when a child's emotionalism is interfering with the rest of the class? I like to provide a "Choice Chair." It's important that this place is seen as a place to go to by choice; it is not a "Time Out" area that a child is sent to for bad behavior. To keep that definition clear, the Choice Chair is near some special "quiet" items, such as play clay, crayons and paper, or "squish bags" (paint or pudding in resealable plastic bags, which are then taped closed for security). When children are struggling to cope with their emotions, they can choose to go to the Choice Chair and use the play items to help them get over the intensity of the emotion. They can return to participate in class whenever they are ready.

The Choice Chair is a great communication device. It says: "I respect your feelings. I am confident you can handle your feelings. Your feelings cannot control the rest of the class, and when you are ready, you can decide to rejoin us." Be sure to acknowledge the child verbally or nonverbally when he or she returns. It's a great opportunity to affirm the child's self-control and growing maturity.

Confidence-Building Communication

To develop positive self-esteem, children need to experience a sense of belonging. They need to feel connected to something bigger than themselves. Because many children come from broken, dysfunctional, or non-nurturing homes, being part of a class at church may be one of the few ways they satisfy this need. Many experts agree that the increase in gangs today is due to a growing number of kids who need to feel a part of something. Gangs may be the only avenue they see to fulfill their need to belong.

Treasured teachers help their students feel a PART of something bigger than themselves by leading them to see themselves as

P—*Privileged to be a partner in God's plan.*

If your children choose to give themselves to Jesus, remind them that they are part of the winningest team in the history of the world! They are children of a Heavenly Father who loves them very much, and he has planned from the beginning for them to participate in his eternal purposes.

A—Affirmed in their position.

Always greet children by name, and show that you are happy to see them. Allow some time for children to greet and interact with each other. Choose a class name to build a group identity. Write a slogan that expresses this group's unique contribution or goals. Create a cheer to build camaraderie. Post pictures of each child in the class, or let them each have space to create their own mini-bulletin boards. Recognize absences with a card or phone call. Undertake some service project your class can do together. (Even preschoolers can do this!)

R—Responsible to each other.

You don't need to carry all the responsibilities of a class by yourself. Enlist the help of each class member. Assign tasks within the class. Let them bring in some of the teaching items. Have the children design and write out postcards. Create opportunities for special service.

When I was a school principal, we had one student with very low self-esteem. Hal was hungry for love, but he went about getting it in all the wrong ways. As a result he had few, if any, friends.

When my children were babies, I kept them in my office until they were old enough to attend school. The students in fifth through ninth grades liked to get their work done quickly in study period or eat their lunch as fast as they could so they could baby-sit for me. One day Hal asked if he could watch my son, Christopher. I hesitated and then suggested that we take him for a walk together. I showed him how to hold Christopher properly and taught him the basics of caring for a little one.

This same child who had often been rough with his peers became a pillar of gentleness! Christopher responded very positively to Hal, who quickly became a favorite of his.

Hal finished his work quickly each day so he could baby-sit Christopher for a while. Christopher often sought out Hal as well. Hal felt that he made a difference in someone's life, and as a result, his self-esteem improved greatly. He became more loving and gentle with the other students. Instead of trying to grab power by being a bully, he found a true place of belonging by being a gentle, loving, caring person.

T—Take-charge kind of people.

Children need to feel that they have some power and can contribute in some way. This does not deny the sovereignty of God; it simply means we show children they have the power to affect their environment. For example, we know that if a child is negative and we continue to reinforce that, we will perpetuate it. If we praise a student's efforts to improve, our comments serve as a catalyst for positive change. Children need to see that they have power to affect others' perceptions of them.

Clearly, our society continues to be plagued by a "victim mentality." A young man robs because he is the "victim" of his parents' poverty. A racist goes on a rampage because he was a "victim" of affirmative action and lost his job to someone else. A student cheats on a test because the teacher "didn't teach it right." These examples of abdication of personal responsibility are the exact opposite of what we are taught to be in Christ (Philippians 4:13).

We can help children develop a sense of "can-do" by looking closely to see what each child is good at and building on that strength. This gives students a sense of the positive use of power in which we utilize God-given strengths to make a difference in the world.

I tell children, "Each of us is really good at some things and really lousy at some things. Sometimes it takes years to find what we are really good at, so we need to keep on trying new things. Eventually we will discover our strengths." Like adults, children tend to focus on their weaknesses, and that leaves them feeling powerless to make an impact in life. They may not realize who they are in Jesus Christ and assess their self-worth by others' perceptions.

When you believe in your students and communicate that to them, you have created an island of security for them. Those children will want to come back each week to the place where they "belong." A Sunday school teacher may provide the only safe island that a child has.

Amy was in my sixth-grade class. She was very quiet the day we studied the passage from Romans 12 on spiritual gifts. After class I asked if she would help me carry my things back to my car.

"What did you think about class today?" I asked as we walked together. Immediately her eyes began to tear. We sat in my car and had a long talk. Amy had never realized that God created people differently for his special purposes. She had always felt second-best compared to her outgoing sister, and as a result, she often retreated from the spotlight.

When she asked me what I thought her spiritual gift might be, I told her

I thought she would make a marvelous teacher. Her eyes lit up.

"Yes," she responded, "I always dreamed of being a teacher." That summer I encouraged Amy to be a teacher-helper with the preschoolers for vacation Bible school. The rest is history. She is a wonderful teacher today!

The charts on the following pages suggest ways you can communicate with children to help them feel confident. Feel free to reproduce these pages to share with parents.

Inner Direction

As you think about these questions, make a note of related personal experiences or Scriptures that contribute to your understanding.

1. When have you seen a child shine in response to a comment from you? What do you think made the communication "click"?

---

2. Set a goal for how often you'd like to affirm a child. How can you keep track of your progress?

---

3. What do you currently do to build group identity for your class? What else could you do?

---

4. State all your classroom rules using positive language.

---

5. What form of communication do you really excel in? Why?

ENDNOTES

1. Benjamin R. DeJong, *Uncle Ben's Quotebook* (Eugene, OR: Harvest House Publishers, 1976), 8.
2. Howard. G. Hendricks, *Teaching to Change Lives* (Portland, OR: Multnomah Press), 84.

Ten Ways to Build Up a Child

1. Express sincere gratitude: "Thank you for helping me!"

2. Encourage the child to share a skill: "Who else could you show how to do that?"

3. Empathize: "I bet it felt great to finish that project."

4. Identify consequences: "You really helped Mrs. Gardner when you collected the left-over bulletins."

5. Appreciate uniqueness: "I never would have thought about it that way."

6. Applaud effort: "I can see a lot of work went into this project."

7. Emphasize growth: "You are making enormous improvements each week."

8. Encourage elaboration: "Tell me more about what happened."

9. Acknowledge good choices: "I know that was a hard decision."

10. Apply scriptural truths: "You were acting in exactly the way Jesus described when he said, 'Do unto others as you would have them do to you.' "

25 Five-Second Encouragers

You make me smile.

I see the care you took.

That looked a lot like Jesus!

You're becoming much wiser.

Thank you for caring.

That was super kindness!

How thoughtful of you!

You really thought that through.

Your creativity is inspiring.

Your enthusiasm excites me.

You are wonderful!

I love being around you.

You handled that beautifully.

You think of great questions.

Awesome, possum!

Way to live God's Word!

What a whiz!

You've been practicing.

You make life fun.

I think you made the right choice.

Couldn't ask for more than that!

Bet you feel great!

I knew you could do it.

Look at you shine!

I can really count on you.

Chapter 8
Desirable Discipline

Treasured teachers understand the importance of discipline
in the classroom and practice "desirable discipline."

No horse gets anywhere until he is harnessed. No steam or
gas ever drives anything until it is confined. No Niagara is ever
turned into light and power until it is tunneled. No life ever
grows great until it is focused, dedicated, disciplined.
—Benjamin R. DeJong, *Uncle Ben's Quotebook*

*"All discipline for the moment seems not to be joyful, but sorrowful; yet to those
who have been trained by it, afterwards it yields the peaceful fruit of righteousness"*
(Hebrews 12:11, New American Standard).

I used to think that if you love children and you love the Lord, you can
go into any classroom, share your message, and everything will be great.
I spent quite a few nights in tears trying to figure out why it wasn't
working! In the process I came to realize what was lacking: an effective plan
of classroom discipline. A class in chaos is not a good place for anyone to
learn anything. Eventually I discovered some key principles of "desirable discipline" that greatly improved my ability to teach and my students' ability to
learn. They work for me; my prayer is they will work for you, too.

The Principles of Discipline

Dedicate your teaching to the glory of God.

We must always remember why we are teaching: We are there for the
Lord. We are not there to win a popularity contest or to see which teacher is
the best at discipline. Keep your focus on him. Begin by dedicating your
teaching to the glory of God.

Demonstrate the love of Christ.

We must learn what it means to demonstrate the love of Christ. First, we must know him personally as Lord and Savior of our lives. Second, we must demonstrate his gentleness as well as his strength. This combination will make you a good disciplinarian.

Give the Holy Spirit dominance.

As believers in Jesus Christ, we have received the gift of the Holy Spirit. He helps us to know what to say as well as when we need to be quiet. Children are used to adults becoming frustrated with discipline and often know just how to "punch our buttons." When that happens, praying for help from the Holy Spirit is the Christian version of counting to ten. Instead of *reacting* on the human level, we *respond* according to the Spirit.

One way to rely on the Holy Spirit when disciplining is to walk and talk as if in slow motion. Walk slowly to a child requiring discipline. As you walk, pray. You will find your response more appropriate because you have placed yourself under the leading of the Holy Spirit.

Let's say a little boy is causing a commotion at one of your centers. Instead of yelling across the room, try the following:

1. Keep your eyes on the child.

2. Walk slowly to him, keeping your eyes on him at all times.

3. As you walk, pray for the Holy Spirit to control your attitude and actions.

4. When you get to the boy, put your face next to his and look into his eyes.

5. If he will not give you eye contact, gently cup his face in your hand and put your face even closer. Some children may look away, and others may close their eyes to avoid looking at you. Because eye contact is so important, wait it out. When you get the eye contact, state your desire: "In my classroom, you may use your hands to love or create or work; you may not use them to hurt. Do you understand?"

6. As you walk away, walk backward, keeping your eyes on the child.

7. Calmly continue teaching.

The calmer and more deliberate you appear, the better your ability to achieve the desired result and the more sensitive you will be to the leading of the Holy Spirit.

Define your discipline style.

It is very important that we model the behavior we expect from our students.

If we arrive late to class, interrupt, talk rudely, or lack self-control, then we can expect our students to exhibit the same behaviors. Our kids learn more from what we *are* than from what we *say.*

When we teach young children, we can often see our teaching behaviors mimicked by observing students playing "teacher." This can be painful if we aren't ready to deal with truth or face aspects of our teaching that are less than perfect.

Be diligent in your preparation.

The more diligent we are in our preparation, the fewer discipline problems we will have. Children always can sense when we are not prepared, and they may try to take advantage of us.

When we rush into class at the last minute without all our supplies, frantically trying to find and set up materials, we invite children to misbehave— especially that one child who always seems to fill up the entire room. We can count on that child to be there early the day we are running late! This student is "everywhere," and the others respond to that. The result is confusion and chaos.

Contrast this scenario with one in which we demonstrate diligent preparation. We arrive before the children, set up the room, organize our visuals and craft supplies. We are calm, collected, composed, in control—and our teaching is more effective. Proper planning produces positive performance!

Use developmental foresight.

We need to take time to study about the children we will teach. Knowing what a typical two-year-old or twelve-year-old is like helps us to have realistic expectations and to teach age-appropriately.

Some teachers think a child is a just child, and if you can teach one age, you can teach another. That is not true. Each age has its own distinctive characteristics; for example,

• Two-year-olds are trying to assert their independence.

• Three-year-olds are not sure they want to grow up and can be somewhat clingy and whiny.

• Four-year-olds are out of bounds! Everything is extreme: They laugh too hard, cry too hard, play too hard, and think that bathroom words are really funny.

• Five-year-olds adore you. If you want to be loved, this is the age to teach! They think their teacher is the center of their little universe. Perhaps God in his mercy and wisdom made five-year-olds to follow four-year-olds so we wouldn't get too discouraged.

• Six-year-olds are very emotional, talkative, and somewhat aggressive. They can be a challenge to discipline because they are trying to achieve their independence again.

• Seven-year-olds are beginning some internal reflection; they can be more pensive and ready for more subjective concepts. They can also withdraw, complain, and whine, and may need extra encouraging.

• Eight-year-olds rush out to meet the world. While they are asserting their independence again, they are also very dependent upon the approval of significant adult figures in their lives. They want approval so much that they study your every response. They may make excessive demands for attention, affection, and appropriate (by their definition) responses from you.

• Nine-year-olds seek approval from peers more than from adults. They very much want to be in control of their world and resist too much adult interference. They may be slow to obey, not so much out of defiance, but in order to feel that they are captains of their own ship. Outwardly, they may appear independent, but inside they worry about things. This worrying may manifest itself in a great deal of complaining.

• Ten-year-olds want to be good and do what is right. It is one of the nicest ages. A recent trend in developmental education is to describe ten-year-olds as very moody. My personal opinion is that external influences, such as television, commercials, and public discussions on AIDS, abortion, and sex, have accelerated the developmental rate in children. Ten-year-olds often manifest signs of an early transition from childhood to adolescence by being moody.

I could go on up the developmental ladder. The bottom line is, to be a treasured teacher, take time to study what is developmentally appropriate for the kids you teach. Your curriculum's teacher guide should provide this for you. If not, suggestions for possible reading are available in the back of this book. *Know thy students!*

Decide and define your basic rules.

A newly hired principal discovered that the walls of the cafeteria were covered with rules. They were so overwhelming that instead of curtailing negative behavior, the rules served as a challenge to students to find new and creative ways to "slip through the cracks."

If we want to have effective discipline, we must keep our rules short and simple. For years now I have been using three simple rules because they cover a broad range of behaviors and they work. You may want to have children recite these rules to you each week:

1. Raise your hand if you want to speak, and wait to be called upon.

2. You may not talk if someone else is talking.

3. Keep your hands on your own body unless you have permission to touch someone else.

End your sentences by dropping your voice. Children don't take you seriously when you end by raising your volume or pitch. Practice talking in a lower, softer voice. You'll have far fewer discipline problems.

Develop your system based on your teaching style.

I've already encouraged you to know your students. Now, teacher, *know thyself!* We need to understand what works for us and stay with it. This may take some trial and error, but we will eventually find our comfort zone. We need to be authentic in how we communicate our desires to our students.

When I taught children in third through sixth grades who were auditory learners and often talked out of turn, I explained to them, "I know that you need to let me know what you think, and talking is a way to express yourself. I want to allow this. However, I am a teacher who likes quiet, and I want to call on you. I am strict about noise levels. I will respect your desires, and you need to show respect for mine." Understanding why I required what I did made the children more willing to cooperate with me.

If you are a fun-loving teacher, you will create an entirely different atmosphere than a Marine sergeant-type. Don't compare yourself to another teacher. Do what works for you. If you see certain behaviors or classroom environments you would like to emulate, learn from them. But remember that your teaching style and temperament affect how you discipline. Be fair to yourself in accepting how God created you.

Differentiate between consequences and punishment.

Once we decide what our rules are, we need to decide what the consequences will be if those rules are broken. Because true discipline is a process of training in appropriate behavior, we must understand that there is a difference between a *consequence* (or effect) and *punishment.* Children may view both as "punishment," but we, as teachers, must distinguish between the two. Children often say a teacher is "mean" when in reality the teacher is "strict." It's OK— even good—to be strict. *Just be fair.*

Children have an antenna for what is fair and just. A *consequence* is a fair response to a behavior that will elicit a more appropriate future behavior. A *punishment* is an often overstated, inappropriate response that creates negative future responses from the child, rather than eliciting a positive change.

Consider these situations:

• The rule is: When we make a mess, we clean it up. Nevertheless, Andy makes a big mess at one center and then moves on to another center without a second thought. An appropriate *consequence* is that he has to go back and clean up the first mess before he plays at the next center. It would be a *punishment* to bring the class's attention to the mess or to not allow him to participate in any more centers for the day.

• Another rule is: We raise our hands to talk during class discussion. Yet Emily continually speaks out without raising her hand. A *consequence* is that she may not talk until she raises her hand and is called on. If she does not raise her hand, she goes to the Time-Out Chair; she may listen but not participate in the discussion until she is invited back to her place. It would be a *punishment* to demand that she write "I will not interrupt" one hundred times.

Essentially, the purposes of a consequence are to

• train appropriate behavior
• preserve the child's dignity
• increase an internal acceptance of responsibility
• increase motivation by facilitating positive self-esteem
• show the student how to work within a system where there is give-and-take
• teach the relationship between cause and effect
• maintain a climate of caring

Steps to Discipline

Disciplining Preschoolers

Let's follow a typical sequence with a child between the ages of two and six. Let's say little Patrick has just hit another child. You should walk slowly and deliberately to Patrick. (Don't yell across the room...please!) Get on his level, look into his eyes, and say quietly, "The rule in our classroom is that we keep our hands on our own body unless we have permission." Then add firmly, "Do you understand?" Use eye contact to show you mean business. Then quietly go back to your teaching, walking backward with your eyes on Patrick.

Hopefully that will be the end of the behavior, but let's assume it continues. Walk to Patrick again, hold his hands, look him in the eye, and quietly and firmly ask, "What is the rule in our classroom?"

He may or may not answer. Regardless of his response, take him to an isolated chair. This is *not* a Dummy Chair or a Bad Chair; it is a *Time-Out* Chair. Put him on the chair as you say, "The rule in our classroom is that you keep your hands on your own body. You hit Sarah, and hitting is not allowed in our classroom. You may sit here until I invite you back to join the class. I want you to look and tell me if you see anyone else hitting in our classroom."

If he stays in the chair quietly, return within one or two minutes. Get on your knees, hold his hands, look into his eyes, and say, "I see that you are sitting very quietly. I am very proud of you. Tell me, did you see anyone else hitting in our classroom? We do not hit in our classroom. You may come back now."

If he did *not* sit quietly, you can do one of three things:

• Require him to sit there until he shows you, by his actions, that he can be invited to return to the classroom.

• Rescind special privileges, such as time with a favorite activity.

• Send a note home to his parents, or call them.

If Patrick continues to disrupt, I strongly recommend that you remove him from the classroom. If the other students see one child successfully dominating your time and attention, they may try the same thing. Arrange to have someone available to help you in such cases—a roving director of Christian education or a department head, for example. Recruit a person who is discerning, loving, and firm to check your classroom once or twice an hour to see if you need a "helping hand."

To sum up, here are the steps to disciplining a preschooler:

1. Go directly to the child and speak firmly and quietly.

2. State the rule first, giving him the benefit of the doubt. ("Rule amnesia" is prevalent among some children.)

3. For the next offense, he must state the rule.

4. Take him to the Time-Out Chair. If he is quiet, you may invite him back within one to five minutes.

5. If he is disruptive, he must stay on the chair until he shows you he is ready to return. Being in your class is a great privilege; assume he will want to be there.

6. Talk to his parents.

7. Have the Sunday school superintendent or someone else take him from the class if his behavior is a significant disruption. This is very important. Children must see that teaching the Word of God is your first priority, and their behavior will not deter you from that goal.

A Word to the Wise

When you talk to a parent about a child, don't show anger. Smile, approach the parent with something positive to say about the child, then say, "I am having a little trouble with...." State the problem, then add, "I wonder if you could help me?" This is far more effective than yanking the child up to the parent and showing your obvious displeasure.

When you approach parents aggressively, they have no recourse but to defend their children. A mother may know exactly what you're talking about when you describe a certain behavior, but she will defend her child because *you* are on the offensive. Or a father may honestly believe that such behavior is not typical of his kid, and he will defend the child against "false accusation." In either case, you lose.

If, however, you approach parents kindly and gently with an "I" statement ("I have a problem..."), they are much more likely to want to help. Believe me, it is well worth the time and effort to make friends with your parents. If they feel you truly care about their children and want what is best for them, they will work with you—and that's a tremendous help.

Discipline in the Primary Grades

For children in grades one to three, we can use the same basic sequence used for preschoolers. For children in grades four to six, however, dignity becomes a critical issue because kids at this stage care deeply about what their peers think of them. *Discipline with dignity* is important for all ages, but we need to be especially sensitive to children between the ages of nine and eleven.

I prefer to talk with these kids about their behavior in private after the class. I try to enlist them as a friend or helper. For example, I might say, "I truly am happy to be your teacher. I believe that teaching the Word of God is so important, I want to be sure that each of my students understands what I am teaching. When you make sounds, poke others, make airplanes from your lesson (or whatever else is causing the problem), I find it difficult to teach. I wonder if you could help me."

Believe it or not, some children are not aware of how much of a disruption they are causing. This is the age when a treasured teacher must be loving and sometimes bluntly honest. But it's best to speak in private so they can "save face."

Dealing With the Difficult Child

Every church in America has at least one difficult child, and often several. It may even be safe to say that the number of these children is on the increase. But there are ways to handle the problems and minister to these kids.

When I do teacher-training workshops on discipline, many teachers share about their problems with certain children. I often say to the teachers, "I will be happy to teach your class for you so you can see these principles demonstrated firsthand." Sometimes they take me up on the offer! That's OK. Modeling is one of the most effective ways to teach.

Who are some of these difficult children, and how can we work with them?

The defiant child

The defiant child is a strong-willed child who wants "control at any cost." Always look in this child's eye. If you discern rebellion or defiance, I encourage you to take strong action. This does not mean to yell, scream, or use physical abuse, but rather to be strong, controlled, and ready to require obedience. Defiance is sin. Strong wills must learn submission to authority. Your manner may produce greater results than your words.

Saying something along these lines has worked for me: "I can see that you have some skills that could make you a leader. You are a very strong child. We need strong leaders in this world, and God may call you to leadership some day. It is important that you first learn to follow, because great leaders first learn to follow.

"God placed me in charge of this classroom. The Bible says we must each come under the authority of those God has placed in charge. I am going to be strict with you because I want you to grow up to be a godly leader God can use in a special way."

Kids respond well to truth. Communication like this brings down the wall that exists between adults and children, teachers and students, and which strong-willed children think they have to continually defy. They respond positively when they realize that we want to work *with* them, not against them—because we care.

It is up to you, as the teacher, not to tolerate defiant behavior. Be sure that you have thought through what you will and will not accept, and have a consequence ready for acts of deliberate defiance.

If younger children refuse to do something, put your body around theirs and literally "do it" with them. For children in kindergarten through second grade, have them sit in the Time-Out Chair until they are ready to obey. Look deeply into their eyes and say, "This is unacceptable to me. I will not allow you to act in this way. Do you understand?" Remember, there is power in eye contact, and it is effective with defiant attitudes.

Always end by dropping your voice. These children, more than any others, will take advantage of you if they think you are weak and acting without conviction. Rebellion is sin and must be dealt with strongly.

The disruptive child

Most disruptive children are disruptive simply because of their learner styles. When that's the case, troublesome behavior can usually be rerouted into more appropriate behavior. Be gentle unless you see *defiance* in their eyes.

For example, Talkers are often disruptive because they love noise and frequently create their own. If the noise-making is subconscious and not an act of defiance (look in their eyes if you aren't sure), gently remind them to be quiet. They usually aren't aware of their disruption and just need humor or a little love pat to help them remember.

Explorers may be disruptive because they simply need to touch. They are driven by this need, and their hands are seemingly everywhere. Be ready to put something into their hands so their touch is constructive, not destructive. They also need to move—so give them appropriate opportunities to do so. Explorers learn best when they are able to feel movement in their bodies.

For my daughter's birthday one year, I arranged "An Old-Fashioned Christmas" party for her first-grade class. That day, I had to deal with a number of instances of disruptive behavior. But when I had everyone get up and move to the Christmas centers where I had activities prepared, the children who had been disruptive became very focused, and the discipline problems stopped.

Afterwards, my daughter and I evaluated the day. She had been my "teacher helper," since it was her birthday. "Mommy, children need to move and touch," she said. "That is when they act the best."

I responded with an inward smile of great joy. "Honey, when you grow up and are a teacher yourself, remember that very important pearl of wisdom," I said. "Mommy believes it, and yet I had to be reminded of it again today."

The Do's and Don'ts of Discipline

Here in a nutshell, are fourteen key "do's" and "don'ts" of effective classroom discipline for treasured teachers:

1. Use direct eye contact.

We must learn to use our eyes to minimize discipline problems. Eyes can communicate so much! Look into the eyes of your students. Communicate that you care. Communicate that you mean business when it comes to discipline. With eye contact, we can help our students feel as though they're an integral part of the class.

2. Exercise diligence.

Muscles become stronger with use—and that includes our "discipline muscles." We must work diligently to find the plan of discipline that works for us, and we must be *consistent* in carrying it out. The time will never come when we can stop disciplining our students; but as we become more proficient and confident in our system, we will reach a point when we no longer have to think about it. It becomes second nature to us.

First-year teachers often lament, "All I do is discipline. I want to teach!" It will come—be patient. Be diligent.

3. Practice detachment.

I almost shudder as I write this because I fear being misinterpreted in this area. I am a "toucher" of children, and I believe in bonding to them with love. But when it comes to discipline, the secret lies in *detachment.* When we remain detached from our students' negative behavior—when we don't react to the many antics they use to detour us—and when we respond warmly and positively to their positive behavior, the negative diminishes and the positive increases.

The adage that says, "I love *you,* but I don't like what you *did"* applies here. Detach yourself from the "riffraff" of your students' disruptions, but don't detach yourself from the love and caring that you feel for them.

Sometimes, when kids try to "push my buttons," I simply raise my eyebrows with a look of mock disbelief that says, "Surely you are kidding me—you don't really want to act that way now, do you?" Sometimes, I simply ignore it. If you react with annoyance to each little antic, you will be like rubber balls bouncing around helter-skelter. Learn to *respond* rather than to *react.*

4. Direct your attention to the little things, and the big things will rarely happen.

Often we teachers let the "little things" go—and then wonder where all the big problems come from. "Little things" may include students leaning back in their chairs, chewing gum, making comments under their breath, or using poor manners.

I find I can resolve most potential discipline problems by redirecting them. For example, I always come to class in an outfit that has pockets. I walk around while I teach, and if I see a student begin to play with little treasures brought from home, I simply pop them into my pockets. The kids have already been told that disruptive treasures go into my pockets and may be retrieved *after* class *with* Mom or Dad.

We live in a world that no longer values good manners. As Christians, let's use good manners in our relationships with children and insist they use good manners with us.

Most problems, I'm convinced, can be stopped before they start. For example, before taking a class into the hallway, it's best to have the students line up quietly in the classroom. Wandering hands can be kept from meandering into trouble by having the kids fold their hands in front of them or behind their backs. This isn't legalism; it's orderliness!

5. Help students determine an internal rather than external focus.

Discipline is a process that requires ongoing training. We want to train our students to be responsible for their own behavior. Teaching responsibility requires an *internal* focus—yet children typically want to blame others instead of assuming responsibility for their own actions.

If you ask, "Where is your Bible?" the answer is likely to be, "My mom didn't remind me to get it," or "We had to leave in such a hurry that I forgot," or "You didn't tell us we had to bring our Bibles." The children's focus is external, pointing responsibility away from themselves.

If clearly stated expectations are not followed, you have an excellent opportunity to help students learn to have an internal focus and take responsibility. Like everything else in training and disciplining children, this requires patience and diligence.

6. Understand that we live in the decade of "me," TV, and the decline of family.

The focus of our society is on "me, me, me," abetted by the pervasiveness of television and the decline of the family. The result is an ever-increasing need for discipline. For many students, church and school are the only environments in which discipline exists.

The goal of external discipline is to develop the internal self-discipline needed to be a disciple of Jesus Christ. Teachers, let us embrace this training process as unto the Lord! Proverbs 22:6 is not a promise, but a *process:* "Train a child [student] in the way he should go, and when he is old he will not turn from it."

This process reaches far beyond the teaching hour, the perimeters of our classroom walls, and our curriculum. It entails training disciplined young people who are not just thinking about "me" and forming their opinions from TV. Rather, these are disciples of the Lord Jesus Christ who are trained to think of others, to form their convictions from the Scriptures, and who are committed to family.

Of course, this process should be occurring in the home. But realistically, it may come only from our teaching each Sunday. When we view discipline from this perspective, we see that we are training children in skills needed for life.

7. Look for ways to dramatize.

When we work with little children, it can help to dramatize. I often say things in an exaggerated manner; for example, "Can you walk back to class so quietly that tomorrow the pastor will ask me, 'Did the two-year-olds come to church yesterday?' I'll tell him, 'Yes, they were here,' but he won't think so because you were so quiet!"

Children enjoy that kind of dramatic talk until they reach about the age of four. Then I change it a little: "Let's see if you can walk so quietly that your teacher (or class helper) won't hear you come in." The kids find their seats without a sound and think they are so clever!

This tactic won't work past second grade, however, so then I simply say, "You *will* walk quietly to class." But using a little drama can make teaching so much more fun!

8. Don't yell—use the bell.

When we yell, children get louder, and the noise level goes up. I recommend getting a bell with a soft tone and making a game out of getting your class's attention. Explain, "This is the 'Freeze Game.' When you hear the bell, turn your eyes to me, hold your hands behind your back, and 'freeze.' After I say what I need to say, you may 'defrost.'"

One of my favorite things to do is to sing to the children. Singing rules or directions to them is such a change that they can't help but pay attention. Before I share something important I always sing, "Eyes on me by the time I count to three." I don't proceed until all eyes are on me. You can't force children to listen, but it certainly helps when you have their eyes focused on you.

Here's another tip: The quieter your voice is, the quieter your classroom will be. Ask any teacher who has ever had laryngitis. Teachers who speak softly have quiet classrooms. The secret is to insist that students be quiet before you speak. Train them in it; it will make teaching so much more pleasant.

9. Deliver an interesting message.

Please don't bore children! Develop a rhythm to your teaching. Teach in multisensory ways whenever possible. Always keep one step ahead of the class. If something isn't working, simply move on to something else.

10. Display humor.

I know, I know. I tell you to be strict, to drop your voice, to speak softly, to insist on good manners, and then I say, "Display humor." The fact is, you can't do this one from the start. You must first establish discipline with your students—then you can begin to have fun.

Enjoy your students. Be willing to be silly and to try new things. If you say or do the wrong thing, don't worry about it. Children love to see you laugh at your own mistakes and say "Whoops!" Be willing to say, "I'm sorry." That alone will teach your students an invaluable lesson.

11. Design your room to meet the needs of your students.

Individual children learn in different ways. Many kids we consider "discipline problems" may be students who simply are not in their comfort zones of learning.

You don't have to pamper your learners and give them everything they want. That would simply feed the "me" focus. However, negative discipline can be eliminated by avoiding situations in which you know children will act up and by designing your room to meet the needs of a variety of learners.

For example, you can provide quiet, structured areas for learners who need that kind of environment, along with centers or free-play areas that meet the needs of others. You may not use each area for the whole class time, but they are available when you need them.

12. Dignify each child.

Find something good to say about each child. Stand at the door, and say something positive and hug or pat each one as they enter. That may be the only encouragement they get all week! If we want our children to fall in love with Jesus Christ, we need to demonstrate the love of Christ in action.

13. Discover the beauty in each child (or pray for God to reveal it to you).

Let's face it: Some children are difficult to love. You may say, "I have tried and tried to find something about this child to love, but I can't." Don't give up. Pray—get on your knees, and ask the Lord to open your eyes. It is amazing what characteristic he will bring to mind or what event he will orchestrate. Maybe you'll drop your papers on your way to your car on a rainy day and be surprised to find that child right there helping you pick everything up. *Something* will happen to enable you to praise, love, and dignify that child. God is love, and he will cause it to happen if you pray.

14. Display godly qualities to the children.

Can you imagine Jesus Christ yelling at a child? You know that's not what he would do! Don't overreact when things go wrong. If your easel gets knocked over or a child spills a tub of paint, it is not the end of the world.

We are in the classroom to teach children about God. Let's take that responsibility very seriously! It's worth repeating: *We teach little by what we say, but we teach most by what we are.*

Let us become more dedicated to being better disciplinarians, and we will love the process of teaching much more. Discipline is inherent to teaching—and an element that can "make or break" a teacher. Pray for God's help. Many gifted teachers have quit because they became weary of the discipline process. How sad! Learning to master discipline is an investment of your time that will reap rich dividends. It will help you become a master teacher—and a treasured one.

Inner Direction

As you think about these questions, make a note of related personal experiences or Scriptures that contribute to your understanding.

1. What role has discipline or lack of discipline played in your life?

_____

_____

2. What is the difference between consequence and punishment in your own words?

_____

_____

3. What is most difficult about maintaining discipline in your class?

_____

_____

4. What strategies of discipline do you believe would make a difference in your class?

_____

_____

5. How is your own temperament reflected in your discipline style? How could you use your temperament more effectively?

_____

_____

Finishing
Well

Chapter 9
Methods and Materials

Treasured teachers teach God's truth with excellence.

A teacher affects eternity; he can never tell where his influence stops.
—Henry Adams

"Your word is a lamp to my feet and a light for my path" (Psalm 119:105)

I once observed an excellent teacher giving a group of four-year-olds a lesson about Creation. His teaching tools were in perfect order. He involved the children; they were completely captivated by the lesson. At one point he moved his hand dramatically through the air as he asked, "And what did God create that is everywhere but not able to be seen?" One bright girl promptly responded, "Germs!"

This teacher had succeeded in his lesson. He had evoked personal involvement. The little girl's answer was not exactly what he wanted, but it was definitely a correct answer! Our personal experience impacts our learning. This child's family had been battling through several rounds of the flu, and I'm sure germs were very much a topic of conversation in that home.

We could sum up the definition of a "treasured teacher" as someone who is called by God to nurture God's children into God's plan for them. Such teachers

- meet learners where they are;
- are spiritually and relationally invested in the growth of their learners;
- teach for eternally significant outcomes;
- build skills that learners can use to learn on their own; and
- help students connect the principles of Scripture to living.

Materials and methods put meat on the bones of those characteristics. We must be eager to try new ideas to reach students. Many years ago I read these words to an old hymn, inspiring my search to find the newest and best ways to teach the "old story":

"New occasions teach new duties,

Ancient values test our youth;

They must upward still and onward,

Who would keep abreast of truth."[1]

Our message is unchanging, but the world is changing at a mind-boggling pace. Technology will not only continue to transform the way children are used to learning; it will actually contribute to young minds being "hard-wired" differently than those of earlier generations. As teachers, we must be constantly on the lookout for methodology that will address these kids' needs.

Every treasured teacher needs a "knapsack" for the journey of learning. In that knapsack, you can put thoughts, ideas, and methods that might come in handy someday. The finest, most carefully developed, most creative curriculum cannot accurately assess your learners. Only you can do that! You know if their families have colds. You know when moms and dads are separating. You know if children are struggling at school. You know if the weather has turned your generally well-behaved darlings into a group that resembles cattle ready to stampede!

If you build an effective knapsack, you will always have a place to go to address these needs. The purpose of this chapter is to give you methods and materials to put in your knapsack. But don't stop here. Let this chapter develop your desire to "keep abreast of truth"!

If you are a new teacher, you may not want to read this chapter now. Use your teacher's manual, and do the best you can to avoid "overload." Come back to this chapter later when you are ready to incorporate some new ideas. Be gentle and patient with yourself as you grow into this exciting call to teach children about God.

For addresses of some of the specific suppliers named in this chapter, check the bibliography at the end of the book.

Teaching With Bible Learning Centers

Bible learning centers are a change of pace from traditional Sunday school activities. They provide self-directed, independent learning experiences and give opportunities for teachers to relate to each student as an individual. Since the most effective learning takes place one-on-one, a center can be the best place to teach!

It can also be the best place to strengthen Christlike leadership qualities and develop positive character traits in energetic children by giving them many appropriate, directed outlets for their abundant energy. A Bible learning center, done well, can emphasize important biblical principles; for example,

- God made each person as a unique individual.
- He created us with a will.
- He expects us to be responsible.
- We're created for relationships with God and others.

In a center, children learn patience ("Wait for your turn in that center"); orderliness ("Yes, you do have to clean it up before you go on"); perseverance ("Keep trying until you get it"); and sharing ("Yes, there are two people in the home center. How can you work together to set the table?"). They also develop problem-solving skills and learn how to make good decisions and choices.

Learning Centers 101

So what exactly is a learning center, and how can you use one in your class? Here's the crash course.

What are centers? A learning center is

1. a method of teaching;

2. a learning activity designed to accomplish specific objectives that can be done without continuous leader assistance;

3. a way of organizing tasks so that learners can make individual choices among a variety of activities and can work at their own pace;

4. a learning situation in which a number of learners may do several different assignments at the same time, choosing to work on one or more tasks appropriate to each individual's ability and interest level;

5. an activity, or several activities, designed to enable an individual or a group to accomplish a specific objective; and

6. a way of organizing material and tasks so that students can make choices and direct their own learning.

Why teach with centers? Essentially, centers are organized learning-through-play times that are great for multisensory learners. They provide a wide variety of experiences through which children use their eyes, ears, and hands to learn. Centers support the "discovery" method of learning; students learn by interacting, and by their own experiences they "teach" themselves.

Who are they for? All children can benefit from centers. They can be set up purposefully to meet the *individual* needs of learners, and kids can progress at their own pace.

Where do I put them? Centers can be adapted to almost any space or teaching environment. Typically, they are set up in designated areas of the classroom and focus on one aspect of the curriculum, such as music, nature, science, or maps. They help to divide the room and provide a familiar and comfortable setting.

When do I use them? Use centers for *part* of the learning time. Remember, they are one of the ways you can teach! Use them to help you emphasize a particular point or goal by giving your learners the opportunity to look at related books, observe plants or animals, draw a picture, or participate in creative play.

Since children often begin coming in ten minutes or so before Sunday school officially begins, have one or more learning centers ready for them so you can make those early minutes count for God. Or if all your children arrive right on time, plan to use the first ten or fifteen minutes for learning center activities.

This can be especially good for active preschoolers who often need a "bridge" between the thoughts and activities they left behind before entering the classroom and the Bible story they are about to hear. A center can provide that bridge by focusing the children's attention on the theme of the day or the background for the Bible lesson.

Preschoolers learn through their senses: feeling, smelling, tasting, seeing, and hearing. We often neglect the first three! Set up centers that make use of all five senses.

How do I begin? Begin with one center, and use it to teach the children about centers in general. Show them the center. Explain its purpose. Spell out rules about using it appropriately. As you achieve success, you can add more.

If you share a room with another group, improvise as necessary. Boxes and piano benches have often served as learning center areas. Use whatever materials you have available, following some of the suggestions in this book. Make a systematic plan for acquiring supplies over a period of time.

Select the centers you will use in each lesson according to the number of children in your class, their particular needs, the number of teachers or helpers available to you, and space and equipment available. If you have only four children and one teacher, select one center idea, and use that as a learning activity for the whole group.

Centers can vary from week to week to fit the aim of the lesson, or they can be established more permanently. For instance, a Home Living Center, a Block Center, and an Art Center can be maintained in the same locations in your room each week.

Here are a few more suggestions for using Bible learning centers:

• Whenever possible, have a teacher or helper at each center to guide the children and lead discussions. The teacher should make suggestions rather than dictate what the children are to do.

• When centers are next to each other, use folding dividers or bookcases to help mark off the distinct areas. If these are not available, don't worry. Most children operate successfully in a flexible situation. Teachers are the ones who may find it hard to function! Keep reminding yourself: *Centers are good for the children...Centers are good for the children...*

• If you have more than one center, let the children choose which one they want to visit. When they have completed an activity at one center, allow them to move on to another.

• Store materials for children to use on low, open shelves or in boxes on these shelves. (Keep inappropriate items on high shelves or out of sight.) Help the kids develop the habit of putting things away when they are finished with them. I suggest coding each item with a dot that matches the dot on the shelf to help the children remember where it goes. Make this the first rule of centers: "We always put things back where we found them and in proper order."

• Do not display all possible materials every time a center is used. Only put out the items that pertain to the day's lesson or theme.

• Make this your second rule: "We use a quiet voice. If we are too loud, we will have to leave the center." Be very strict about this one! Activity excites children, and your classroom can become loud and chaotic quickly. If you require only quiet, "inside" voices, the noise level stays manageable.

• Have the children review the rules before class begins. Invite them in a quiet voice to go one at a time to the centers. If things get too rowdy, use a signal (ring a pleasant-sounding bell, play a chord on the piano, sing a song, or blink the lights) to get their attention, and then quietly redirect them or review the system.

• Circulate continually to assist children, manage discipline, and maintain order. Be a "pillar of peace" as you circulate. Whisper instructions, gently encourage, praise, pray, touch, affirm, and assist. You will be amazed at how much order your very presence can achieve.

• Use a bell or other signal to conclude the learning center time. Give a warning signal several minutes in advance so children can begin putting things away and cleaning up. Then give the final signal to call the children to the next activity.

Attend to the details of order. Little things do lead to bigger problems.

As you can see, Bible learning centers require a little extra thought and planning. But the responses of the children make them well worth the effort!

Sample Centers for Preschoolers

1. Worship Center

Purpose: Provide an orderly area for children to be quiet and reflect on God's Word.

Procedure: Use a small table or shelf; add a pretty cloth, a Bible, and maybe some fresh flowers.

Make sure your Bible is age-appropriate and tailored to the interests of your class. For preschoolers, this means using a picture Bible, such as

The Beginner's Bible: Timeless Children's Stories by Karen Henley (Zondervan Publishing House, 1997)

The Gold and Honey Bible by Melody Carlson (Multnomah Publishers Inc., 1997)

The Early Readers Bible: A Bible to Read All By Yourself by V. Gilbert Beers (Multnomah Publishers Inc., 1996)

The Hosanna Bible by Angela Abraham (Word Books, 1993)

The Pray and Play Bible for Young Children (Group Publishing Inc., 1997)

This kind of center works well with elementary-age children, too. Move to Bibles that have a third-grade reading level, some pictures, and helpful reference keys; for example,

The Kids Life Application Bible (Tyndale House Publishers, 1998)

The New Explorers Study Bible (Thomas Nelson, 1998)

The Kids Quest Study Bible (Zondervan Publishing House, 1998)

The DK Illustrated Family Bible by Claude-Bernard Costecalde (DK Publishing, 1997)

Presentation: Encourage the children to see how quietly they can pray or read God's Word. Be reverent. Remember, children are mimics!

2. Nature Center

Purpose: Encourage children to appreciate the incredible world God has made, and help them feel like a contributing part of the class by bringing in "treasures" from home to share with the other children.

Procedure: Let the children bring in any nature items that they have collected, or limit it to a single item such as rocks or shells. Allow them to discover and explore *carefully* on their own. This is a low-maintenance center because you don't have to do anything. The children do the work and assume ownership of the center.

Presentation: Encourage the class to be thankful to God for his wondrous creation. Help them to treat each other's items with great care and respect.

3. Books Center

Purpose: Encourage children to love books and to read or look at books that reinforce the Bible lesson.

Procedure: Put books related to the curriculum lesson in baskets or on shelves in a corner. Find nice big pillows or rocking chairs to make the book corner warm, cozy, and inviting. Show children how to open books, turn pages properly, and return them correctly. Use big books whenever possible. (A large selection is available from Group Publishing.)

Presentation: Teach them to be respectful of books and to treat books with care and love. They need to know that books are our friends! Help them to fall in love with reading.

4. Art Center

Purpose: Provide different creative mediums for children to express what they've learned from the lesson.

Procedure: Place a table, chair, and a variety of art mediums in this center, and invite students to create an art representation of the lesson. Add an easel if your budget and space allow.

Presentation: Let kids be creative! Through open-ended projects, encourage children to come up with their own ideas and interpretations. Also plan a structured art project that involves clear and definite steps to completion.

5. Bible Puzzle Center

Purpose: Allow the child to see, touch, and complete Bible lesson puzzles.

Procedure: Provide a variety of age-appropriate puzzles on a shelf or in a puzzle rack. Puzzles that have a *knob* on each piece are especially good for preschoolers; this trains the pencil-grip reflex and makes the puzzle easier for little fingers to handle. Large puzzles that must be put together on the floor are excellent as well since they involve shoulder action as well as hand-eye coordination. Judy Instructo puzzles are a good choice; these floor puzzles teach Bible concepts and are bright, colorful, and childproof. Children can stomp on the pieces (no, you shouldn't allow it, but it could happen!) without breaking them. (For older children, add jigsaw and other more difficult puzzles.)

Presentation: Show the children how to do a puzzle correctly: (1) Look at the picture to get it in your "mind's eye." (2) Take the pieces out carefully and set them right side up. (3) Put the picture together again.

6. Home and Family Center

Purpose: Allow young children to role play real-life situations. (Preschoolers see work and play as synonymous!) Cultivate valuable concepts like serving and sharing.

Procedure: This center can be as simple or as elaborate as your space and budget allow. It works as successfully with a box and some plastic dishes as with a complete manufactured play kitchen, living room, and dining room. Use the character-trait application of the lesson to help children play in a directed manner.

Presentation: The key is *attitude.* Home-living skills are what we are teaching! Give directions and ask questions, such as

- Show me ways we can *show love* to our family members.
- What are some ways we can *give* to our family members?
- Show me ways we can *serve* one another in our family.
- What are some things that family members *share* with one another?
- How can we *show that we care* when we invite people to our home?

7. Listening Center

Purpose: Provide a place for children to learn through listening. This center is a special comfort zone for the auditory learner.

Procedure: Show the children the proper care of tapes, recorders, earphones, and volume controls. Provide a tape recorder and tapes or a CD player and CDs.

Presentation: Show the children how to use the listening center—where to find the tapes or CDs, how to turn the machine on, how to adjust the volume, how to use earphones. If you don't have earphones, come up with some clear guidelines for volume control. Teach the kids about the proper use and care of these resources.

8. Drama Center

Purpose: Allow children to dramatize Bible stories or real-life situations. Most children enjoy this center—they love to "make believe" and pretend.

Procedure: Have church members donate old clothes, hats, gloves, and purses. For a Bible Drama Center, simply save old bathrobes and towels.

A Puppet Center can be elaborate or very simple. A table on its side or a cardboard box can serve as a puppet stage. Or a stage can be constructed out of PVC pipe and curtains with a hem. Puppets can be made from bags or socks. Don't be limited by limited resources!

Presentation: Give children the freedom to be creative. But keep an eye on them. This center will get children more excited than others; you may have to limit it to two children at a time.

Elementary Centers

The older your students are, the more creative you have to be with learning centers. Older children become more set in their particular learning styles and gravitate to the centers that specifically meet their learning needs. Keep changing or rotating the centers you select so that learning is always fresh and tailored to individual learners.

Here are some suggestions for centers for elementary-age kids. Remember: Don't attempt all of them at one time. Change or rotate them regularly.

Worship Center	Bible Maps Center
Audiovisual Center	Game Center

Book Center	Drama Center
Cooking Center	Evangelism Center
Art Center	Music Center
Woodwork Center	Missions Center
Computer Center	Listening Center
Prayer Center	Puzzles Center
Bible Time Line Center	Parables Center
"You Were There" Center	Creative Center

The ABCs of Bible Learning Centers

To conclude, here are some key points about the use of centers in the classroom. I call them the "ABCs" of Bible learning centers.

A—Attitude is important in meeting students' needs.

B—Before you begin, think through the details.

C—Children can care for the centers if trained to do so.

D—Discipline is important to establish before you begin.

E—Evangelism is the part of your centers that counts for eternity.

F—Finishing what you begin is an important principle to teach.

G—Godly character is our first priority.

H—How we introduce a center includes stating its purpose and procedures.

I—Individual learning needs are best met with learning centers.

J—Jesus is to be lifted up in all we say and do.

K—Kindness should permeate the atmosphere.

L—Learning is multisensory for the young child.

M—Manners, please!

N—Nature centers are fun; children can bring in priceless treasures!

O—Open your mind, heart, and spirit to new ideas.

P—Parables can be "hands on" too.

Q—Quiet voices help everyone learn more effectively.

R—Respect each child's work.

S—Space does not need to be a limitation.

T—Time-Out Chairs may be needed if children choose to disrupt.

U—Understand that learning takes time.

V—Verses can be memorized in a Memory Center.

W—With God, all things are possible!

X—(e)Xamine your attitude, and pray.

Y—You can do it!

Z—Zealously guard the rights of the individual learner.

Teaching in a Small Space

If you have limited space, you can still create an exciting multisensory experience for your students by keeping hands-on items in a box and then setting the items out on the floor when you want to use them. I know one teacher who had to teach in the church kitchen, so we put together a box and then arranged the items on the countertop in her "classroom" each Sunday. After class she boxed the items up and took them home.

If you have space for only one shelf in your room, you can set your items on that shelf. Invite the children one at a time to go to the shelf and select an item, take it to their place, complete it, and put it back.

Activities in a Box

What kinds of items can you put in the box or on the shelf that will appeal to preschoolers? You can get many ideas from the descriptions of preschool centers. *Puzzles* with large pieces that can be put together on the floor are excellent, as are table-top puzzles with knobs. *Clay* is good because it can be used to teach almost any lesson. It is a wonderful item to have available for your kinesthetic learners in particular. If you make your own (see the recipe on p. 142), you can keep it soft for a long time by putting it in an airtight container. *Books* are always good for any age, and most children love them. Be sure to take time to teach the children the proper use and care of these valuable treasures.

"God's creations," or little items that represent the seven days of creation, are fun to keep in a basket. As the children play, you can encourage them with statements like, "That's right, God made the sun. God made the sun, moon, and stars on the fourth day of creation." Little Christian Supply is an excellent source for these kinds of items. Or you can simply go to a toy store and buy baby toys in sun, moon, and star shapes, along with plastic farm or zoo animals. Remember, little children will want to taste the "creations" as well as touch them, so make sure the items are larger than a 50¢ piece.

For elementary-age students, fill your box with age-appropriate Bible games that you make up or purchase in a Christian supply store. Add Bible maps, Bible time lines, Bible books, and an assortment of art mediums.

The key is to have an assortment of materials on hand so you can keep changing the procedure of your teaching. This way, the children each will eventually be taught in the way they learn best.

Of course, kids don't say, "Oh, now the teacher is teaching for the Talkers. Next we'll have to do centers for the Explorers, but eventually we'll get back to teaching the 'right' way for us Lookers." When you vary your teaching methods, a rhythm is established that children learn to trust. They can't articulate *why* they feel relaxed and *why* they trust you to meet their individual needs, they just do!

Materials for Preschool Teachers

In chapter 3, we listed many methods and materials that can be used to bridge to a specific learner's style. (See p. 42.) However, most children don't develop strong learner preferences until they approach the age of seven. That means that preschool students will benefit most from exposure to a variety of teaching methods that help them explore the world God created through each of their senses: sight, hearing, smell, taste, and touch.

Here are some ideas to help you stock your classroom with items that will give you maximum flexibility for multisensory preschool teaching.

Art Overview

The key phrase for any preschool art experience is "process over product." This means that the experience of doing a project is more important than the final outcome. "Cookie-cutter" crafts that provide a model and then give children all the pieces to create the project are much more satisfying for the teacher than for the child. You may want your students to complete such a craft from time to time (maybe as a service project or gift), particularly if you want to teach a lesson on following directions. Even then, children learn more when they supply more creativity than just choosing the color of the construction paper.

Here's what you need:

Cover-ups are important for any activity that might get messy. Use old adult T-shirts or trash can liners with holes cut out for a head and arms.

Glue in bottles is for squeezing and watching the puddles form. Most young children don't have the coordination to apply squeeze glue properly. Glue sticks are great! If you need to use liquid glue, thin it with water and let children paint it on with brushes or cotton swabs.

Scissors are tools that are fun to work with and help develop small motor skills. However, they're not really art equipment at this age.

Paper of all kinds is great fun. Keep drawing paper, newsprint, construction paper, tissue paper, finger-paint paper (or wax paper), butcher paper, old file folders, odds and ends of wrapping paper, and recycled paper on hand. Paper can be folded, drawn on, painted, colored, cut, or torn.

Make easy collages by using sticky paper rather than trying to apply glue to the pictures or objects going on the page. Tape the adhesive paper to the table and have children lay the collage items on.

Hint: Paper on a table slips! Tape it down to help young children control it.

Crayons, markers, pencils, and colored pencils are for making marks and drawing—not for coloring in spaces until children are about four years old. At four, most children are ready to take on the challenge of coloring pictures. Before that, coloring pages are just a place to make marks and explore colors. In fact, with younger children, coloring pages are most effective if you let kids add tactile objects or stickers to them rather than asking them to color them.

Finger paint allows children to use their own "equipment" to create art. In addition to the commercial products, you can finger-paint with such items as baby lotion, liquid starch, pudding, shaving cream, and nontoxic hair gel. Any of these can be colored with food coloring or unsweetened powdered drink mix to add color and scent. Paint on a slick paper, such as waxed paper, or on the table top itself. Make a print of an "original" by laying a sheet of plain paper over the top, pressing down, then removing it.

Stamps with washable-ink stamp pads can be fun. No stamp pad? Pour some tempera paint on a damp sponge and work it in.

Glitter can actually be dangerous if inhaled, and glitter glue has many of the same disadvantages as other forms of liquid glue. If you want to provide the experience of shaking something on paper, try cornmeal or salt in a shaker jar. If you want to use glitter, have the children indicate where they want it to go and you or an adult helper can apply it.

Clay, goop, and goo are wonderfully flexible supplies you can keep on hand all the time. Most modeling clay is too firm for preschoolers to use comfortably. It's easy to make your own. See pages 142 and 143 for some recipes you may want to try. There are many other homemade clays that are equally fun.

More Materials

Blocks can be used to construct all kinds of wonderful places in the imagination, and they can also bring the places you talk about in your Bible story right into the classroom! Children can construct the tower of Babel, the road to Jerusalem, the stable where Jesus was born, the ship Paul sailed in, and more!

A good set of commercial classroom blocks is a luxury. There are many other building alternatives that serve the same purpose:

• sponges (for *quiet* building blocks)

• well-sanded wood scraps

• stuffed paper bags or lunch sacks sealed with masking tape

• milk cartons (Cut the tops off of two milk cartons, and slide one down into the other. Cover them with decorative adhesive paper if you want.)

• grocery boxes stuffed with newspaper and taped shut (Pudding boxes make excellent small blocks; cereal boxes are great for larger projects.)

Another idea is to use a desktop publishing program to create a three-dimensional box pattern. Print multiple copies on card stock. Cut them out and cover them with clear self-adhesive paper (or laminating film). Fold the boxes and stuff them with tissues; then seal them shut with glue or tape. Make soft blocks by substituting self-adhesive felt for the clear covering.

Blankets and sheets, in addition to providing comfy seating areas, can be useful for all kinds of things. Try these:

• Lay out a blanket to protect the floor from a messy project.

• Use a sheet as a "parachute." Hold the sheet at the edges to raise and lower it in time to the rhythm of praise music.

• Use a blanket as a "clean-up" or "transport" assistant. Kids can load the blanket with items that need to be put away and pull it along the floor to the supply shelf.

• Create a "story tent."

• Let children make Bible costumes from small blankets.

Play Clay Recipe

1¹/₂ cups flour

1 teaspoon powdered alum

1 cup boiling water

1¹/₂ cups salt

1 teaspoon vegetable oil

Food coloring

Mix dry ingredients. Add oil and water and stir vigorously with a wooden spoon. Add food coloring as desired and knead. This makes 2 cups of dough. Do not double this recipe for large amounts, but mix several recipes instead. For reusable play clay that will keep for several months, store in a tightly covered container. Objects made with these ingredients dry to a hard finish overnight. Put clay in a basket with some cookie cutters and a small rolling pin, and you have a complete center.

Edible Play Clay

1 cup nonfat dry milk

¹/₂ cup creamy peanut butter

¹/₂ cup honey

Knead all ingredients together. For dark dough, add ¹/₄ cup cocoa powder. Note: If this dough is too sticky, you may add 1 tablespoon of flour or powdered sugar at a time until the dough reaches the desired consistency.

Sculpting Clay

For each child you'll need:

1 slice soft white bread with crust removed

1 teaspoon white glue

A drop of dishwashing liquid

Crumble the bread into fine pieces (or put through a food processor). Mix crumbs with glue and dish-washing liquid. Store in individual resealable bags.

Goo

2 cups white glue

$1\frac{1}{2}$ plus $1\frac{1}{3}$ cups warm water

Food coloring

4 teaspoons Borax (found in the laundry section)

Mix the glue with $1\frac{1}{2}$ cups warm water, and add several drops of food coloring. In a separate bowl, mix Borax with $1\frac{1}{3}$ cups of warm water until Borax is dissolved. Pour the first mixture into the second. Don't stir. Wait a few minutes; then remove the solid from the liquid. Knead the solid, and store it in an airtight container. Dispose of the liquid.

• Use blankets on the floor to define groups or to identify an area you want to confine the kids to.

• Have an indoor picnic.

Boxes and laundry baskets can have many uses, as well. Ever noticed how at birthday parties just as many children play with the boxes as the toys? Boxes are tremendous items to keep on hand, especially the big ones that children can climb into. Laundry baskets offer some of the same flexibility. They can become push vehicles, boats for water stories, or containers for gathering leftover loaves and fish. Here are some other ideas for boxes.

• Make a Mary and Martha's house. Cut windows and a door from a walk-in size box.

• Create a tunnel. Cut the bottom and top out of a large box. Cut along one edge from corner to corner. Form a triangle with two sides overlapping. Tape the triangle in place with duct tape. It's great fun to crawl through the tunnel to get to story time.

• Make a rotating three-dimensional gallery station, posting children's artwork on each side. You can also cut a paper-size square out of each of the four sides to make four frames for separate pieces of art. Paint the box with spray paint to match your classroom color scheme.

• Make miniature sandboxes. Fill a small box with sand or salt, and place it inside a baking pan with sides. Provide scoops and kitchen utensils to play with or plastic toys to create a scene. How about Moses leading the people out of Egypt? Put pieces of cloth around pocket-sized action-figure dolls, and tie them with burlap string to make the costumes look "authentic." The children each can move their own figures through the sand as you read the Bible lesson.

• Create theme boxes, asking children to place items that "belong" together in the same box.

Books, as we've noted before, are great for all ages. Children love all kinds of books—and not just commercially produced ones. Try these:

• Make class books. Ask everyone to contribute a page and a thought about the lesson or theme you are presenting. Staple the pages together, and add a construction paper cover.

• Make lesson review books. After you've finished with the lesson's teaching aids, tape or glue the visual aids on one side of a two-page spread in a large spiral-bound art pad. On the other side, write the things the children can remember about the story. Later, the children can look at the review book on their own, or you can read their recollections of the story to them.

• Make thematic accordion books by cutting strips of construction paper and folding them accordion-style. On the front, write a theme, such as "God Made Everything." Attach a sticker or stamp of some item in nature on each accordion section of the paper. Children can "read" these picture books to one another.

• Create class picture books by affixing a photograph of one of the class members on each page. Write a short biography of the child below the photo.

• Make sensory books by adding fabric, fragrance, sandpaper for rough spots, and other touchable items.

• Cut photos from magazines that show children expressing different emotions, and paste them on pages in a notebook. Use this book to "find a face" that expresses the emotion of a Bible story character.

• Make a birthday book for each child's birthday. Have children draw pictures and tell you something that they like about the birthday student, which you can then write on the bottom of their pages. Use birthday wrapping paper to make the cover for the book, and send it home with the birthday child.

Dolls, puppets, and stuffed animals are the toys that allow children to process and practice Bible concepts in play. Try to provide a large variety. If storage is a problem, hang a net in a corner of the room to act as a hammock for your "resting friends." Try to have dolls representing various ethnic groups, whether your group is diverse or not. This helps children become familiar with all of God's people. Try some of these additions to your collection:

• Make small, bendable dolls from chenille wires. Make a loop in the center of the wire. Bend the wire back from each side to form arms, twist the wires together to form a waist, and separate them again to form legs. Add hair by tying individual pieces of embroidery floss or yarn around the loop. Wrap the limbs and body with embroidery floss, or glue on tiny felt clothes.

• Make character dolls for storytelling by gluing or taping a picture to a block.

Try the following kinds of puppets, adding a variety of creative facial features:

• Sock puppets

• Clothespin puppets. Decorate a three-inch Styrofoam ball to look like a face. Cut it in two so that the eyes, nose, and upper lip are on the top portion of the ball and the rest of the mouth and chin are on the bottom portion. Glue the top of the ball to one side of a spring-type clothespin and the bottom to the other side. Move the mouth by pressing on the open end of the clothespin.

• Pop-up puppets. Punch a hole the size of a straw in the bottom of a foam cup. Mount a picture of a person or animal on the top of a straw. Insert the straw into the cup so that the figure cannot be seen until the straw is pushed up.

• Envelope puppets. Fold an envelope in half widthwise. Carefully cut a slit along the fold line, being sure to cut the top layer of the envelope only. Children can put their thumbs inside the bottom pocket and the other four fingers inside the top pocket. Decorate these puppets to be people or animals.

• Sticker-stick puppets. Attach stickers to the ends of craft sticks. Dip the stick puppets in salt to cover whatever adhesive is not holding the sticker to the stick.

Remember: Children *love* puppets. They don't have to be "perfect" in order for children to use them and enjoy them. Shy children will often tell "Little Lambie" what's going on with them when they won't tell the teacher.

Be creative. I often use a puppet to tell the Bible lesson or to ask questions afterwards. And I find that "Bible Bear" is a great disciplinarian. "Bible Bear says he won't be able to stay with us today unless everyone is listening quietly," I might tell my students. If they are too loud, Bible Bear begins to slowly move away—and the room instantly becomes hushed. With Bible Bear by my side, I rarely have to discipline the children!

Older children love puppets, too—although they would never admit it. Occasionally I go into the upper-grade classes and ask the kids or young teenagers to help me make some puppets or to write some puppet shows and perform them for the younger children. They are always happy to volunteer to "help"!

Fun With Music

You don't have to be musical to enjoy music with preschoolers. They care more about the enthusiasm you demonstrate than the notes! There are some wonderful professional releases that teach Bible verses, stories, and character traits to young children, such as those by Steve Green, Miss Pattycake, Mary Rice Hopkins, Rob Evans, Psalty, and more. It's worth it to invest in a low-cost CD player rather than a tape player; instead of having to struggle to cue the tape for the song you want, you can go right to it on the CD by punching a number. These precious seconds saved can mean the difference between a class in chaos and one on-task and between using the most convenient song and the one that's most appropriate for your lesson.

You can also let the children sing along with some of the excellent music videos available from your local Christian supply store. Many of these videos give children motions to do along with the song, making it a truly multisensory experience.

When you are teaching new music to children, try the following techniques:

1. Sing a line, and have the children echo the line back to you.

2. Sing a line, and when you approach a key word, hold the note without saying the word. Have the children sing the missing word.

3. Say the lyrics, pausing for the children to fill in a missing word.

4. Talk about the meaning of the song. For global thinkers, this is an important step that helps them identify the big picture. Singing becomes communication rather than mere word-calling.

5. Use "directed repetition." (This is my personal favorite.) Rather than singing a song over and over in the same way, tell the children to sing it in a certain style: "like a baby," "in an opera voice," "like a very old man," "like there's someone in the next room who needs to hear you," or "like a lullaby." The list of possibilities is endless—and the children get to repeat the song over and over for memory without getting bored. Work on voice quality later.

Sometimes, if it is really important to learn a song, I ask for a directed repetition as the children are doing some other activity. This provides "interval reinforcement," the strongest kind of reinforcement for committing something to memory. (This strategy works with Scripture memorization as well.)

Finally, try some of the following homemade rhythm instruments to use as you sing:

• Mitten castanets. Use those partner-less mittens to make an instrument by sewing a one-inch button on the hand and a half-inch button on the thumb.

• Bell shaker. Place several jingle bells (available at craft stores) inside a plastic soda bottle. Glue the lid on.

• Pie plate tambourine. Punch holes around the rim of an aluminum pie plate. Thread a chenille wire through the loop of a jingle bell, then attach the wire to the pie plate. Twist the wire about ten times and cut away the excess. Add more bells around the plate.

• Bleach bottle drums. Cut the bottoms from two bleach bottles, leaving four- to six-inch sides. Fit the bottoms together so that each end of the drum is solid. Depending on the rigidity of the plastic, you may have to cut one or more slits in the outer bottle to accommodate the inner one. Wrap colored electrical tape around the sides to hold the drum together. These "drums" can be played with little hands or a wooden spoon.

• Ribbon rainbows. For silent movement with music, take a yard of each of six different colors of half-inch ribbon. Hold the ribbons together and tie a large knot in the center. (You may need to tie several knots on top of one another.) Holding the streamers at the knot, children can wave them overhead, down low, in front, and to the side as you direct them.

Small Motor-Skill Builders

Besides offering the many different types of interlocking blocks and puzzles that are commercially available, you can help preschoolers develop their small motor skills by letting them try some activities from this potpourri of options:

• Use kitchen tongs to grasp and pick up cotton balls as an activity to go with any story about a shepherd caring for sheep.

• Use paper punches of all sizes and design around the edges of construction paper sheets to create mats for mounting important pictures.

• Create puzzles from sheets of craft foam (available at craft stores). Trace patterns on the foam, carefully cut out the shapes with a blade, and let the children put the pieces together. You can even use figures from your resource pack as the puzzle pieces. Simply glue them to the foam and cut out around them. After you remove the pieces, cover them with clear self-adhesive vinyl.

• Glue pictures to the inside of a meat tray. Cut the foam into puzzle-shaped pieces. Store the pieces in plastic bags.

• Make individual flannel boards by attaching flannel to a piece of cardboard using spray adhesive. Children can play with all kinds of flannel graph figures or felt pieces.

• Using a cookie sheet and magnetic figures, let children re-create stories.

Story Strategies for All Ages

I suppose some great storytellers are *born*—but I think more of them are *made*. Telling stories is an important part of being a treasured teacher. You can learn to be a great storyteller by working on these five keys:

- Know your story.
- Use your voice wisely, varying tone, pitch, and volume to communicate meaning.
- Believe in the significance of the story.
- Watch your pacing, and never tell a story too fast.
- Respond to your audience.

To get the most out of a storytelling experience, listeners must become involved in the story, feel the emotions described, and be able to "place" themselves in the story. You can help your learners accomplish these goals by being flexible in your approach to storytelling and adopting some basic strategies that can be applied to all kinds of story experiences.

Your first job is to focus the students' attention on the story experience so that they listen with their minds engaged. You can do this in several ways:

1. Set the purpose for listening. All students listen better if you give them some sense of direction about what to listen for. Do that by

- *focusing the learners by style.* For your Lookers, you might set the purpose by saying, "Look for words that describe the place the story happened." For your Talkers you might say, "Decide what you would have said to..."; for your Explorers, "Imagine what else might have happened"; for your Thinkers, "Count how many times the writer used the word..."

- *focusing the learners on general listening.* Say things like, "Raise your hand each time you hear a name in the story." "Turn your hand over when you hear something you might have done." "Hold a finger up when something happens that you don't understand. Put the finger down if something else in the story helps you to understand."

- *focusing the learners by telling them how they might use the story.* "How many of you have a family? Listen to how Joseph learned to deal with his family." "Listen to this story. We'll use details of the story for the craft we are doing afterwards." "Listen to the story so that you can retell it when I'm done."

- *focusing the learners by presenting a point of view.* Have the children listen for details that support or fail to support that point of view.

2. Ask good questions. The art of good question development can be applied to all areas of teaching, but it is especially important as you try to help children connect the Bible to their lives. No matter how creatively you craft your lesson, it will be the questions you ask that will help your students draw meaning out of the material you present.

Make sure your curriculum provides questions that go beyond recall, and write additional questions in the margin of your teacher guide. Here are some strategies for creating questions that really make children think:

• Ask questions that can't be answered with a yes or no. If you can't think of another way to ask the question, be sure to follow up with "Why?"

• Ask questions that can't be answered by a single word.

• Ask questions that have more than one right answer.

• Ask for more details.

• Ask how children arrived at their conclusions.

• Ask questions of opinion.

• Ask questions that require emotional engagement, such as, "How do you think so-and-so felt?" or "How did it make you feel when…"

• Ask the learners to formulate questions!

3. Help learners think things through.

In addition to asking good questions, you can use a number of strategies to help your students think things through in a way that will cement the lesson and encourage life application:

• Wait. Give kids plenty of time to answer, and don't let one student answer for the rest.

• Think out loud to allow your students to listen to you process your thoughts. This can be a powerful modeling strategy and also gives students another window for observing your authenticity. You can also think through something in a faulty way and ask students to identify where you went wrong.

• When children veer from a biblical basis for their thinking, explore how the Bible relates to what they are saying. You may need to keep a concordance handy for these occasions.

• Let students give their answers to partners rather than to the whole group.

• Ask children to summarize what their classmates say to encourage learning from each other.

Flexible Storytelling

As we mentioned, how you tell stories can be tailored to meet the needs of a variety of learner styles.

For the Looker

1. *Storyboard.* To build a storyboard, begin with a wooden frame (like a window frame) with glass or Plexiglas in it. It can be any size, depending upon how many people will need to see it. Ours has been used for up to five hundred people. Place the framed glass on rollers so it can be moved easily. Attach fluorescent lights across the top of the back of the frame, and put a skirt around the bottom so you will not be able to tell someone is behind it. (See the diagram below.)

On white butcher paper cut to fit the framed glass, make a light pencil drawing that will illustrate your lesson. Tape the paper to the glass.

With the lights of the storyboard on, have an assistant who is *behind* the board trace over the pencil drawing using thick colored markers. The teacher stands in front of the storyboard and teaches the lesson, which corresponds to the markings that are "showing up" on the board. The lights prevent the children from seeing anything other than the drawing as it appears.

Storyboards are great for grown-ups, too. At my pastor's request I've taught lessons in "big church" with the storyboard. More than a few grown-ups have told me they get more out of the sermon when Mr. Storyboard comes to visit!

2. *Flannel or magnetic figures.* Place figures on a flannel or metal board display as they are mentioned in the story.

3. *Chalk talk.* Draw figures or portions of figures as you tell the story.

4. *Clip-and-tell stories.* Cut out paper figures as you tell the story.

5. *Sandbox stories.* Place three-dimensional figures in a mini-sandbox as you tell the story.

For the Talker

1. *Response stories.* As you repeat a certain phrase in the story, the listeners call back a response.

2. *Echo stories.* The listeners echo a phrase back to you on cue.

3. *Take-part stories.* Distribute parts of the story to the listeners (written on cards or cut-out shapes). When you come to a part of the story that corresponds to a listener's part, ask the listener to read it out loud.

4. *Sound-effect stories.* Analyze the story for sounds that might be associated with it, or choose a sound association for different characters in the story. For example, in the Christmas story, the shepherds might be represented by the bleating of sheep (there are wonderful little toys that can provide this sound effect), the angels by the clink of a spoon on a glass of water, and Mary by a segment of a lullaby on tape. Play (or have the listeners play) the sound effect each time the story mentions the corresponding character.

5. *Rhyming or rapping stories.* Chant or sing the story. Sometimes it's best to do this for only a small portion so that it augments the story rather than overpowering it. For example, every time David is mentioned in the story of David and Goliath, chant, "Killed the lion, killed the bear, God's in charge, so better beware!"

For the Explorer

1. *Motion stories.* Have listeners respond to defined parts of the story by performing an action, such as rotating their arms in a slingshot motion for David, hitting their foreheads with the ball of their hands for Goliath, and raising their forearms to their chests for the Israelite army.

2. *Muscle stories.* Ask the children to listen to the story standing up, and have them mimic the large muscle movements you use as you tell it. The story

of creation is very effectively told in this way as you present the expanse of the universe with wide open arms; divide the land and the sea with big cutting motions; and toss the stars into the sky.

3. *Clay modeling stories.* Give each student a lump of clay, and have them copy your own sculpting as you tell the story.

4. *Mime.* Have students silently create their own story actions as you tell the story.

5. *Body sound-effect stories.* This is similar to the sound-effects story for Talkers except that all the sound effects must be made using children's own bodies. Stories with storms in them are wonderful candidates for this technique!

For Thinkers

1. *Sequence stories.* Divide the story into small segments, and write the segments on cards. Read one of the cards; then hand it to a child, and have the child stand in a designated place in the room. Read the next card, and have the class decide if this part of the story happened before or after the first. Give that card to another child. Once the story is sequenced, with the children holding the cards and standing next to one another in the right order, review the whole story.

2. *Monologues.* Monologues appeal to Thinkers because they are told from the single point of view of a character who appears to be an expert.

3. *Mysteries.* Give your class many story details, and allow the students to try to formulate the outcome. In teaching Bible truths, this can be quite challenging, since children have to apply their own knowledge of God's ways to the details.

4. *And then...stories.* Stop at strategic times during the story, and have the children find the facts about what happened next.

5. *Outline stories.* Present a brief outline of the story in written form, and give a copy to each student. As each part of the story is told, the children check off that part of the outline.

Music as a Tool to Teach the Bible

We already talked about fun things to do with music and preschoolers. But I want to take this a step further and apply it to children of all ages. I believe music is one of the best ways to teach concepts to kids. If they can sing something, they will remember it. They can learn anything faster when it's put to music. So how can we use music in our teaching?

1. Hymns of the faith

Teaching children the great classic hymns of the Christian faith connects them to a very important part of our heritage. But children don't always learn hymns as quickly or easily as they do other songs, and they may balk initially when you introduce them.

A great way to begin is to use the Kids' Praise! 7 tape or CD by Word Incorporated titled, "Psalty's Hymnological Adventure Through Time." This fun production makes hymns "come alive" for children, and they love it! As I write this, I am getting our young elementary students ready to perform this musical for our church. It is wonderful to hear children in grades one through three learning and singing hymns—and having a great time!

I believe it's reasonable to teach children one hymn a month. Your particular church probably has its favorites. In case it doesn't, here's a suggested plan for your first year that parallels holiday celebrations:

January: "It Is Well With My Soul"

February: "And Can It Be"

March: "Christ the Lord Is Risen Today"

April: "I'll Go Where You Want Me to Go"

May: "Savior Like a Shepherd"

June: "Oh, How I Love Jesus"

July: "Doxology"

August: "Stand Up for Jesus"

September: "Trust and Obey"

October: "Holy, Holy, Holy"

November: "This Is My Father's World"

December: Christmas carols

2. Scripture verses set to music

One of the most effective ways to teach Bible memory verses is to put them to music. There are some great commercially available examples, such as the Deen-O recordings by For Kids Only and Brentwood Music's "Scripture Rock" by Troy and Genie Nilsson. It's important to choose music that reflects your children's musical tastes.

An added dimension is to also teach sign language. You don't have to be trained in American Sign Language to do this: You can simply add some motions that help the children to remember the words. If you are blessed to have someone in your church who signs, you can enlist their help.

To teach a Bible verse with sign language, follow these steps:

• Sing the verse with the children.

• Say it and sign it.

• Sign it in silence.

• Then sing and sign together.

The children will have a much higher level of retention this way. And, as a plus, they will be very quiet and responsive. They love to do this!

3. Character traits

Christlike character traits, such as honesty, kindness, and joy, are important concepts to teach our students, and music helps plant these concepts down deep. The kids ponder them repeatedly as they hum or sing the songs over and over. Many excellent children's tapes and CDs are available that teach good character. Just browse through your local Christian music store.

Teaching Bible Memorization

Most Bible curriculums provide their own Scripture memorization program. Rarely are the various programs coordinated, even though students might participate in several. Sometimes children get one verse to learn at Sunday school, another one at their Wednesday night club program, and still another at their Christian elementary school. Many children are put on "overload," and they can't master any of it.

I believe it's better for children to master a few verses well than to have a general knowledge of many. For that reason I developed the following Bible Memory Program for both our school and church:

Age 2: Twelve short verses—one per month

Ages 3 and 4: ABCs of Bible Memory from Association of Christian Schools International

Kindergarten: Selected verses from Proverbs; Lord's Prayer

Grade One: Books of the Bible; Ten Commandments

Grade Two: Verses describing the fruits of the Spirit (for example, in September, two to four verses on love; in October, joy; in November, peace, and so on)

Grade Three: Large passages and verses from Psalms

Grade Four: Verses on sharing the gospel; the Beatitudes

Grade Five: Verses and passages from the Book of John

Grade Six: Guidelines on holy living from Galatians, Ephesians, Colossians, and Philippians

Another idea for grade six is to have each child select a book of the Bible and recite the entire book before the church before moving up to junior high. It is impressive to do, hear, and experience! Obviously, you would discourage the selection of Leviticus as the book to memorize, but James or Philippians is wonderful!

You can develop a program for your church or school based on the priorities you have, but I encourage you to always surround it with activities that help students understand the significance of the verse or passage for their lives. Be sure they understand every word. When I have children say memory verses for me, I also have them paraphrase the verse so I know they can really use the verse in their lives.

Don't make the memorization process a test, consciously or subconsciously, of which child is the most spiritual! Some learners simply memorize better than others. And since the rewards of knowing Scripture by heart are internal, don't link memorization to rewards of candy or treats.

Regardless of the system you select or develop, the bottom line is this: *Get your kids to internalize God's Word!* Jesus used his grasp of Scripture to defend himself against the attacks of Satan, and your children can, as well.

What an adventure teaching is! The exciting part is that *you* end up learning more than your students. Any time I have wanted to learn more about something, I have tried to teach it so someone. As I research the subject, ponder it, pray about it, I grow. But the real learning occurs when I *give* it to someone else. It is truly more blessed to give than to receive (Acts 20:35)! Keep in mind that the same is true for your students. Prepare them to share. Teach them to be living witnesses.

I pray that this book will be a friend that will stay with you for many years as you learn, stretch, and try new things in the ministry to which you have been called. We *grow* into treasured teachers—teachers who teach with an eternal focus. As we walk with Jesus, as he grows us into the Christians and teachers he wants us to be, we find we always have more to share with the children we teach and love.

Inner Direction

As you think about these questions, make a note of related personal experiences or Scriptures that contribute to your understanding.

1. Which ideas presented in the chapter could be most easily integrated into the lesson you are teaching this week?

_____

_____

2. Are there strategies in the chapter you have used either as a teacher or as a student? What are your memories of the experience?

_____

_____

3. Are there materials around your house or yard you could easily use in a center? What are they?

_____

_____

4. Think of a particularly memorable story you were told. What made it memorable? What characteristics of the storyteller remain in your mind?

_____

_____

5. Since we learn so much from the process of teaching, what are some ways you can involve your learners as teachers?

_____

_____

ENDNOTE

1. James Russell Lowell, "Once to Every Man and Nation," stanza 3.

Chapter 10
Communicating Christ to Kids

Treasured teachers know that leading children to Jesus Christ and helping them to grow in the Lord is the most important work they will ever do.

A halfhearted attempt to cultivate our children's spiritual development will lead to young people with halfhearted commitment to God.
—Benny and Sheree Phillips, *Raising Kids Who Hunger for God*

"Go therefore and make disciples of all the nations, baptizing them in the name of the Father and the Son and the Holy Spirit, teaching them to observe all that I commanded you; and lo, I am with you always, even to the end of the age" (Matthew 28:19-20, New American Standard).

Some dear friends have two very spiritually mature daughters, but their third child doesn't seem to be taking things quite so seriously. Even though the little girl is only three, the two big sisters have been really working on her. Laura and Anna Grace asked Alyssa, "Do you know how you can get to heaven?"

"Sure," the three-year-old responded.

"How?"

"On an airplane!"

To help her begin to reflect more deeply about her potential spiritual plight, they asked with great dismay, "Alyssa, do you want to go where there is fire all the time? What would you do there?"

Not to be dismayed, Alyssa replied, "I would just roast marshmallows!"

I don't think we have to worry about Alyssa's future. She is being raised in a strong, Christian home with Christlike parents. However, we do need to worry about the children of the world in general. We must put the issue of salvation at the top of our teaching priorities if we are to teach with an eternal focus.

Understanding Salvation

Leading others to Jesus Christ lies at the core of this book. *A treasured teacher teaches for transformation through Jesus.* All the other teaching we do remains at the periphery if students are not transformed by the knowledge of Christ and changed from the inside out.

For a long time I was one of those people who thought if I went to church and was a "good" person, I would, of course, go to heaven. I was an adult when I first clearly understood the Gospel and received Jesus Christ as my personal Savior. Then my life began to be transformed, and a hunger to know Jesus and his Word began to take root.

My personal experience has made me especially committed to making sure children know the Scripture, hear the Gospel, and understand what it means to be changed into the likeness of Christ. Since children are literal learners, the concept of belonging to God can be approached from many angles. This shows us how dependent we are on the Holy Spirit to help us teach God's message to kids.

The lesson of Nicodemus being "born again" in John 3:1-21 can pose a particular teaching challenge. I had every angle covered (or so I thought!) to ensure my class's understanding. "Did this mean that Nicodemus came out of his mommy's tummy again?" I asked the kindergartners. "What does it mean to be 'born of the spirit'?"

That night a parent called to tell me her daughter accepted Christ with her father. They were thrilled because she had been able to clearly articulate her decision, and they believed she truly had an experience with the Lord. However, when bedtime came, she began to cry. "Since I was born again, do I have to sleep in my crib again?" she asked. Back to the drawing board!

Because I am aware of the danger of teaching that is not connected to a personal relationship with Jesus Christ, I constantly ask children questions, such as

• I guess you will be going to heaven since you are coming to Sunday school, right? (No? Why?)

• Think of a time that you were really, really good. Now, do you think Jesus would let you go to heaven because of *how good* you were that day? (No? Why?)

• I am praying for each of you to know Jesus and to be able to go to heaven. Will my prayers get you to heaven? How about if your mommy and daddy pray this for you? (No? Why?)

Finally, the most important question:

• If Jesus came back through the clouds today, do you think he would take you with him to heaven? (Why? Why not?)

Continually provide checks like these to be sure your students understand that salvation is a personal decision that no one can make for them. They must *know* that they are sinners and *invite* Jesus Christ to be their Lord and Savior on their own. Often a child wants Jesus but does not yet understand these principles.

Coming to grips with our sinful nature is a prerequisite to the Christian life. Sometimes children will be able to tell you all the "bad" things their friends or family members have done but will look you right in the eye and tell you that they haven't done any of those things. Some children may think that since they haven't committed the "big-time sins," they really aren't sinners.

A child needs to be able to discern the difference between being sorry for getting caught and being sorry for sin. I use many stories and analogies to help children deal with this major issue. When we realize that Romans 3:23 ("For all have sinned and fall short of the glory of God") really means *each one of us,* then the process has begun.

The next hurdle is learning to deal with the sin inside of us by confessing it and asking forgiveness. My friend, Sue Bohlin, illustrates this for children by taking a bar of soap and writing on the soap wrapping, "If we confess our sins, he is faithful and just and will forgive us our sins and purify us from all un-righteousness" (1 John 1:9). The soap serves as a practical reminder that just as we need to wash our bodies to be physically clean, we must confess our sins to stay spiritually clean.

Tools for Sharing the Gospel

Many helpful tools are available to help you present the Gospel to children. Often, Sunday school curriculums weave opportunities for confession into their lessons. A number of wonderful organizations—Child Evangelism Fellowship, NavPress, and Association of Christian Schools International, among others—have also published materials you can use. (See the bibliography for the addresses of resources named in this chapter.)

Statistics tell us that 85 percent of the people who make a commitment to Jesus Christ do so *before* the age of eighteen and 62 percent before the age of twelve. Is there any stronger motivation for mastering this skill as part of your teaching ministry?

So where can you begin if you are new at sharing the Gospel with kids?

1. Share your testimony

Telling others about your life and how you became a Christian is one of the best ways to share the Gospel because you already know it! It is your personal experience, and you probably won't forget it, even if you are a little nervous. Sharing how you became aware of your sin and your need for a Savior prompts a similar response in others because of the authenticity of your story.

2. Mark or memorize key Bible passages.

Key Scriptures that explain salvation can be guiding lights for others. Study the verses below. Find the ones you would be most comfortable working with, and mark them in your own Bible with a highlighter, bookmark, or ribbon.

To make children aware that they need a Savior because of their sinful nature:

• Isaiah 12:2: "Surely God is my salvation; I will trust and not be afraid. The Lord, the Lord, is my strength and my song; he has become my salvation."

• John 3:16-18: "For God so loved the world, that he gave his only begotten Son, that whoever believes in him shall not perish, but have eternal life. For God did not send the Son into the world to judge the world, but that the world might be saved through him. He who believes in him is not judged; he who does not believe has been judged already, because he has not believed in the name of the only begotten Son of God" (NAS).

• John 5:24: "I tell you the truth, whoever hears my word and believes him who sent me has eternal life and will not be condemned; he has crossed over from death to life."

• Romans 3:10: "There is no one righteous, not even one."

• Romans 3:23: "For all have sinned and fall short of the glory of God."

• Romans 6:23: "For the wages of sin is death, but the gift of God is eternal life in Christ Jesus our Lord."

• 1 John 5:12-13: "He who has the Son has life; he who does not have the Son of God does not have life."

To help them know that God loves them very much:

• Luke 19:10: "For the Son of Man came to seek and to save what was lost."

• John 3:16: "For God so loved the world, that he gave his only begotten Son, that whoever believes in him should not perish, but have eternal life" (NAS).

• Ephesians 2:8: "For it is by grace you have been saved, through faith—and this not from yourselves, it is the gift of God."

To explain that Jesus took the punishment for their sin:

• 1 Peter 2:24: "He himself bore our sins in his body on the tree, so that we might die to sins and live for righteousness; for by his wounds you have been healed."

• 1 Peter 3:18: "For Christ died for sins once for all, the righteous for the unrighteous, to bring you to God. He was put to death in the body but made alive by the Spirit."

• Revelation 1:5: "...to him who loves us and has freed us from our sins by his blood."

3. Use a "Gospel acrostic."

I am indebted to Child Evangelism Fellowship for this model I've often used:

G—God is love

John 3:16: "For God so loved the world, that He gave His only begotten Son, that whoever believes in Him should not perish, but have eternal life" (NAS).

O—Only perfect Son

Galatians 4:4: "But when the time had fully come, God sent his Son, born of a woman, born under law."

S—Sin

Romans 3:23: "For all have sinned and fall short of the glory of God."

P—Precious blood

Revelation 1:5: "...to him who loves us and has freed us from our sins by his blood."

E—Everlasting life

Acts 16:31: "Believe in the Lord Jesus, and you will be saved—you and your household."

L—Let Jesus be your Savior

Ephesians 2:8-9: "For it is by grace you have been saved, through faith—and this not from yourselves, it is the gift of God—not by works, so that no one can boast."

Here's another acrostic I call the ABC Plan of Salvation:

A—Acknowledge that you are a sinner.

B—Believe that Jesus gave his life for you.

C—Confess your sin.

D—Decide you will serve Jesus.

E—Express your trust in him.

4. Try the bad news/good news approach:

Here's the bad news:

You are a sinner (Romans 3:23).

The penalty for sin is death (Romans 6:23).

Here's the good news:

Christ died for you (Romans 5:8).

You can be saved through faith (Ephesians 2:8-9).

Jesus is Lord (Romans 10:9).

You are his child (John 1:12-13).

Sharing With Specific Learners

We've discussed in great detail how different children have different learner styles. I've often gotten a good response from kids when I've used Gospel-sharing materials from Child Evangelism Fellowship and Acorn Children's Publications, in particular, because they provide opportunities for young children to use all of their senses as they learn about what it means to believe in Jesus. How can you vary your approach to reach individual learners?

Because Lookers want to *see* things, you can

• Show them key verses in the Bible.

• Show them a book that shares the Gospel, such as Child Evangelism Fellowship's *Wordless Book.*

Because Talkers wants to *hear* and *talk* about things, you can

• Share your testimony with them.

• Let them talk about times they have "goofed up" in life.

• Read Scripture passages aloud with great voice inflection, and discuss what they mean.

Because Explorers want to *touch* things, you can

• Provide Child Evangelism Fellowship materials such as the *Wordless Book* and the "Gospel Glove."

• Let them look up passages in their own Bibles or follow along with their fingers as you read.

• Have them retell the message using toys, crafts, or other materials.

Because Thinkers want the *facts,* you can

• Give them the straight Gospel message.

• Show them resources that explain the Gospel in a sequential and analytical way.

The Time Is Now

If sharing the Gospel message is a new experience, begin today to prepare yourself for this most important mission. As you prepare, you will find yourself growing spiritually. Remember, different techniques work for different teachers. Some teachers may want to look up verses and write them out. Others may want to discuss the Gospel message with a friend first in order to internalize their plan and get comfortable with it. Still others simply need to step out and *do* it. Do what you need to do, but do it now!

Many years ago I had the opportunity to hear Dr. James Dobson and Gary Bauer discuss their 1990 book, *Children at Risk.* They said they believed a civil war was raging in the United States over the hearts and minds of our children—and I had to agree. After that, whenever I spoke at Christian education or ministry conferences around the country, I talked about this civil war and about the corridors of choice our kids faced. I asked my audiences, "Who will be there for the children as they walk down these precarious paths?"

I shared that the teacher's job was more important than ever in the 1990s. Not only were we battling the overt influences of evil, such as drugs, sex, and violence, we were battling insidious evils such as the New Age movement and humanism. We needed to take a stand, regardless of where we taught or what we taught.

Now, as I am updating this book, we are on the brink of the new millennium. What do I write and say *today?* Things have gotten far worse as we have progressed through the last decade of the twentieth century. Who would have foreseen the pervasiveness and power of the Internet? our president's sex life described in graphic terms on prime time and in every newspaper? *Nightline* calling to interview me about "the response of children to the presidential sex scandal"?

More than ever I am committed to training people to be treasured teachers who teach in the light of eternity. I am completely *sold out* to sharing Jesus Christ with children in every arena possible.

We must be the moral compass for our children as they drift in a sea of moral ambiguity, bombarded daily by a culture that has no moral absolutes. Conduct and character are contagious to children, and we must always remember that they learn more from who we *are* than from what we *say*.

I recently accepted a position as national director of education for the Every Church a School Foundation. My job is to work with schools and churches around the country and particularly to show churches how to become more involved and effective in education.

One point I frequently make is that back in the not-so-distant past, when our country was at its strongest morally, it was *assumed* that parents were responsible for the education of their children; any church or public responsibility was merely *delegated*. I believe we must empower parents once again to become involved in their children's education. In that sense, every church (and home) is a school, and every parent is a teacher.

We *must* get involved! If parents are called to be "salt and light" in the public schools, let us support them. If parents are called to home-school, let us provide a canopy for them. If a church wants to start a Christian school, let us help them.

Many, many Christian parents and teachers across America are concerned about the future of their children. That's good—we need to be concerned. Frankly, I'm worried about those of us who *don't* seem to be concerned. It shows the powerful effect of the desensitization of our culture—the old "frog in the kettle" paradigm. We must combat the culture if we are to save our children from the moral decay that permeates it.

Truth is essential—the absolute truth of the Word of God. Truth is not just what you can get away with! We must teach our children this principle, and we must have it modeled by our leaders. As treasured teachers, *we* are leaders. Character does count. Morals do matter. Integrity is the issue. God's Word is the only true way to teach this to our students.

Of course, we must never force salvation on children; we must gently lead them to it. Jesus, our Good Shepherd, gently leads *us,* and he is our example.

As Douglas Wilson, author of *Recovering the Lost Tools of Learning,* said at a training session at our school, "We cannot have 'McThoughts' or 'education-to-go.'" Education must have depth to be effective. We have not reached the goal of true Christian education until the children in our care have personal relationships with Jesus Christ. We can provide excellent teaching that is Christian, but it is only when our students put their faith in Jesus that the true teachings of Christ can transform their lives.

Inner Direction

As you think about these questions, make a note of related personal experiences or Scriptures that contribute to your understanding.

1. What steps led to you becoming a follower of Christ?

_____

_____

2. What are some parts of your story you feel comfortable sharing with your students?

_____

_____

3. Which model of sharing the Gospel are you most comfortable with?

_____

_____

4. What verses or process have you committed to memory to help you share the Gospel?

_____

_____

5. If you have not already done so, mark your Bible to share the Gospel.

_____

_____

Teacher
Training Sessions

Introduction to the Teacher Training Sessions

The following sessions are provided to help you develop motivational training for the teachers you work with.

Because we have emphasized the importance of modeling throughout this book, we wanted to give you two model lessons incorporating the same considerations about learner styles and specific methods we've encouraged you to use. The first session shows what kinds of learners or methods we had in mind when we developed each activity. You might classify the activities differently than we did, and that's OK. The important thing is that you get in the habit of really thinking about how to structure your lessons to benefit your learners. When you do this, you actually become more of a facilitator than an instructor—and that's what active learning and treasured teaching are all about!

For more model training sessions, see the FaithWeaver Director Manual, 1999-2000 by Group Publishing.

Session 1
A Matter of Style

(to be used with chapters 1 and 2)

Overview: In this session, you will help teachers learn to identify and appreciate their own unique styles as well as those of their students.

To Prepare: Collect four different kinds of phones. The lesson uses the examples of a plain touch-tone phone, a cordless phone, a cell phone, and a modem (a picture of a computer will do, or use a multiline phone), but you can use any four different phone designs if you don't have access to all of the ones we mention.

You could collect more and use them to decorate tables. (Add silk flowers or office supplies to make a centerpiece.) Mark the ones you plan to use for the session with a post-it note attached to the bottom of the phone. Plan to have one of the phones ring as part of your Engage activity, or record a ringing phone before the session.

You will also need

- Photocopies of the Informal Teaching Style Inventory found on page 17
- Pencils or pens
- The following three questions written on newsprint and posted so that they can't be seen until you're ready to use them:

  What do you like best about teaching?

  What kinds of students are most pleasurable for you to teach?

  What makes a perfect class session?

- A piece of newsprint, a marker, and masking tape for each of four groups
- Four Bibles
- One copy of the handout on page 173 for each teacher
- Enough eight-inch squares of white paper and scissors for everyone
- A DingDong snack cake for each participant

Engage (for Relaters and Talkers; interactive learning):

Welcome your participants. Ask them to form pairs and sit knee-to-knee. Ask the partners to share who was the first president they remember. Give

169

them about thirty seconds to share; then call for their attention with the ringing phone sound you prepared in advance. Ask them to share what the first phone they remember using was like and where it was located. After about two minutes, ask people to share some of the more interesting recollections they heard.

Ask: **How many people recalled a phone in their kitchen? in the bedroom? some place else?**

Make a generalization from their answers, such as: **If I were to judge by your answers, I'd have to say that the [kitchen] is the appropriate place to have and use the phone. Would you agree that the [kitchen] is the best place for a phone? Why or why not?**

Say: **A telephone is simply a device that allows people to communicate important (and sometimes not so important!) messages. There's no magic place for them, and today there are many different forms that telephones take.** Show the four different phones you will use during the lesson. Have the participants point out the advantages of each.

Say: **Like a telephone, teaching is a device through which we attempt to communicate important messages. Because of our own experiences, we may have a strong idea about the form that teaching should take. But just as there was some difference of opinion about what the "right" kind of telephone was, there is bound to be some difference of opinion about what the "right" way to teach is. Just as we saw some distinct advantages to different kinds of phones, there are distinct advantages to different kinds of teaching.**

Say: **To help us get a handle on the way we each function as teachers, let's explore some broad categories of teaching styles.**

Explore (for Organizers and Thinkers; intrapersonal intelligence):

Pass out copies of the Informal Teaching Style Inventory and pencils. Explain how to mark the inventories, and allow between five and ten minutes for each participant to complete and score the inventory. Suggest that those who finish before the time is up think about and list times their style has clashed with that of a learner and what they learned from those clashes.

When they have finished, say: **For right now, we're going to call the people who scored their highest score in the first column the "Cordless Phone Communicators."** Pick up your cordless phone, and place it in an area where all those participants can gather. **People who scored highest in the second column are "Modem Moderators."** Continue placing the other phones to designate gathering places. **People who scored highest in the third column are our "Touch-Tone Teachers," and those who scored highest in the fourth column are "Cell Phone Scholars."**

Have the participants move to the area of the room indicated by their inventories to discuss the questions you wrote before class on newsprint. Ask them to come up with a group answer for each question and to write those answers on their own sheet of newsprint, posting it on the wall when they are finished. Allow about ten minutes for discussion, calling for the whole group's attention with the ringing phone sound.

Ask everyone to look at the posted answers and to identify elements that all the styles seem to have in common. Then note the things that are unique, and read the descriptions of the various teaching styles from pages 15-18.

Say: **So our "Cordless Phone Communicators" are our Relaters. They like to keep in touch with people as they go about their tasks. Our "Modem Moderators" are our Researchers. They like to get facts from a variety of sources and are inclined to be our "techies." Our "Touch-Tone Teachers" are our Organizers. They are rather traditional. Have you ever noticed you can always depend on your touch tone phone? It never gets lost or misplaced. Our "Cell Phone Scholars" are Doers, always flexible and on the go.**

Say: **After hearing these descriptions, if you feel that you really are better characterized by another group, you may move now.**

Expand and Express:
Part A (for Lookers and Talkers; cooperative learning groups):

Ask each group to select a reader, a recorder, and a reporter.

Have the reader look up Psalm 139:13-16 and 1 Corinthians 9:20-22 and read them to the group. Then have the groups relate these two passages to the process of teaching. Have them use leftover space on their newsprint to draw an image that represents a classroom where the teacher is committed to applying both those scriptural principles. Allow about five minutes; then ask the reporters to share the significance of their visual.

Part B: (for Lookers, Thinkers, Organizers, Explorers, Doers)

Give everyone a copy of the handout on page 173.

Say: **There are five basic categories that come together to form each person's specific learning style.** (These categories are adapted from the Dunn and Dunn Learning Styles Model designed by Drs. Rita and Kenneth Dunn.) **These factors never come together in quite the same way; that's what makes all of us quite different! But understanding this complexity will help you to develop strategies that will make a difference in your teaching.**

First, we need to understand that there is no right or wrong preference as far as learning goes, but we can hinder our students from learning if we insist that our own preferred style is the only acceptable choice.

Have the participants fill in the blank lines as you describe the characteristics of each category. (If you know you are going to be short on time, fill in the blanks before photocopying the handout, and allow everyone to look it over as you speak.)

The environmental category choices include:
- **quiet and background noise**
- **bright or soft lighting**
- **warm or cool temperature**
- **formal or informal room design** (such as desk and chair vs. bed or floor)

Circle your preference for each of the environmental factors.

Now let's look at emotional factors:
- **motivation** (what makes a person become involved)
- **persistence** (the ability to keep trying)
- **responsibility** (the ability to act with accountability)
- **structure** (the degree of need for external task definition)

Sociological preferences include
- **prefer to work alone**
- **prefer to work with one other person**
- **prefer to work in a team**
- **prefer to work in the presence of authority**
- **prefer variety of groupings**

List a child in your class who shows a preference for each of the sociological characteristics.

Physical preferences include

Environmental

_____
_____
_____
_____

Emotional

_____
_____
_____
_____

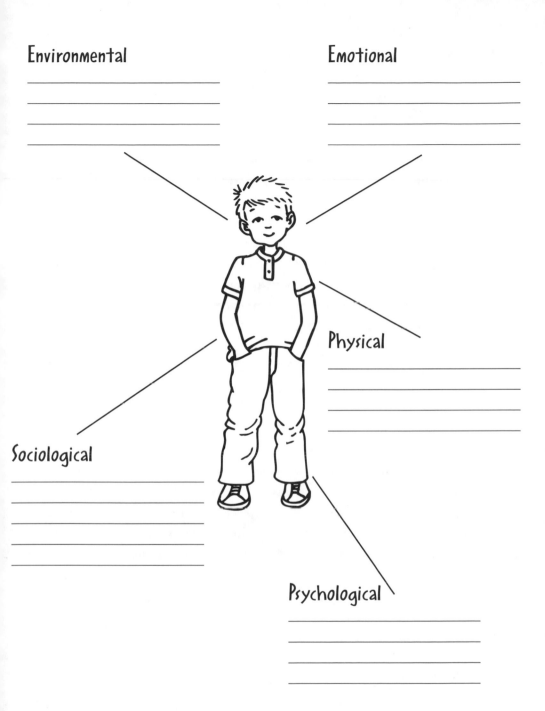

Physical

_____
_____
_____

Sociological

_____
_____
_____
_____

Psychological

_____
_____
_____
_____

- **perceptual strengths** (For an explanation, see p. 15.)
- **need for food in order to think**
- **time of day the learner is most alert**
- **degree of need for movement or activity**

Psychological factors include
- **Analytic or global pattern** (deductive or inductive thinking)
- **hemispheric preference** (See pp. 31-32.)
- **degree of impulsivity**
- **readiness** (a complex set of psychological factors based on both developmental and circumstantial conditions)

Pass out the white paper and scissors. Have the participants fold the paper a few times in whatever way they want to. Ask them to make a different-shaped cutout in the folded paper for each of the factors listed on the handout, cutting into the sides but not cutting an entire folded seam. There should be a total of twenty-one separate cuts. When the group has finished cutting, have them unfold their papers and rotate around the room comparing their "snowflakes" to find the one in the group most similar to theirs. These two people will become partners.

Evaluate (for Talkers; interpersonal intelligence, interval reinforcement):

Ask the partners to share one thing that was impressed or reinforced for them during this training session. Then have them share one teaching challenge in which they are struggling to appreciate the uniqueness of a student. Have them pray for each other and trade snowflakes to remind them to hold one another up in prayer during the following weeks. Ask them to commit to making at least one phone call to their partner over the next month to reinforce the learning experience.

Give each participant a DingDong—the snack that most closely resembles a telephone ring!—to eat now or take home.

Session 1
Practical Planning
(to be used with chapters 3, 4, and 8)

Overview: In this session, you will help teachers learn to evaluate their curriculum in order to prepare lessons that teach God's Word in a way every learner can connect with.

To Prepare: Collect multiple maps and pictures of children. Put the children's pictures on the maps, with big red arrows pointing to each child. Use these maps to decorate the room. Plan to play children's vocal music in the background as teachers arrive. (Make sure children are doing the singing!) You may wish to have some helium-filled balloons at each table, as well, to set an atmosphere that will remind them of children.

Ask your teachers to bring their teacher guides, or provide enough copies of a single lesson for each teacher to have one.

You will also need

• Copies of the Lesson Planning Guide from page 176

• Bibles

• Additional copies of *Touching Hearts, Changing Lives: Becoming a Treasured Teacher*

• Pencils, pens, or fine-tip markers

• Newsprint and marker or chalkboard and chalk

• Three-ring binders (optional)

Welcome the group, and explain that during this session you will be attempting to make maps or lesson plans that will "lead" you to each of your learners. To do that, you need to devise a route to each of your learner style clusters. Your curriculum gives you the basics, but you may need to add to the plans in order to be most effective with your students. Instead of having the whole week to plan and prepare, you will be rushing through a lesson in a single session.

PLAY-ful Planning Guide

Pray and Ponder the Passage
Learn the Lesson
Analyze Your Aids
Yield Yourself to be Used

Scripture Reference: _____

Single Focus: _____

<table>
<tr><td rowspan="2" style="writing-mode: vertical-lr">Learner Styles</td><td>Looker (Preschool—Sight)

Visual/environmental element?</td><td>Talker (Preschool—Sound)

Interactive element?</td></tr>
<tr><td>Thinker (Preschool—Strong application questions)

Thought-provoking questions?</td><td>Explorer (Preschool—Taste, smell, touch)

Hands-on/active element?</td></tr>
</table>

Supplies Needed:

Step 1

This session is designed to be unique for different groups of teachers. Since the goal is to work with the specific curriculum your teachers are using, form groups of teachers who use the same manual, if feasible. Otherwise, form groups of teachers who work with kids in close age ranges.

Ask each group to select an upcoming lesson from their teacher manual (or distribute the lesson you will work through together). Distribute copies of the Playful Planning Guide and pencils or pens.

Ask the groups to look up the Scripture indicated for the lesson and read it aloud. Say: **The first step of effective lesson planning is to pray and ponder the passage. I'm going to ask your groups to do exactly that. When you have finished reading the passage, please take some time to pray together that God will direct your group's thoughts as we work to make sure our lessons are as strong as they can possibly be.**

Step 2

Pass out copies of *Touching Hearts, Changing Lives: Becoming a Treasured Teacher.* (If you don't have enough copies for everyone, have the teachers share within their groups.) Have the participants look at the characteristics of the various learner styles on pages 33-35.

Ask each group to look over the lesson as it is written in their teacher guide. Decide where each recommended activity most closely fits on the learner style grid and write it in the appropriate quadrant of the Lesson Planning Guide. Remind them to also identify a single point and the necessary supplies. Give the groups approximately fifteen minutes to complete this part of the session.

Step 3

Have the groups each discuss where the lesson seems to be particularly strong and potentially weak. They can see this graphically by looking at the grid they've just filled out. Ask a reporter for each group to tell the whole assembly about their findings.

Then have the groups go back to work to fill in the gaps, using the information provided in chapters 3 and 8 as resource material. They may also come up with ideas on their own. Remind them to add the necessary supplies to the list. If a group finds that their lesson is strong in every area, have them look for ideas to expand the activities or to apply the lesson a little better to specific learners in their classes. Allow twenty to twenty-five minutes for this activity.

Step 4

Write the words "Engage," "Explore," "Expand," "Express," and "Evaluate" on newsprint or a chalkboard. Give a brief summary of each phase of the lesson as found on pages 66-71.

Ask each group to determine whether the lesson has an effective progression through the Engage, Explore, Expand and Express, and Evaluate portions of the lesson. Remind them that most curriculums have more activities than they will have time to complete. Ask:

• **What factors do you consider when you are picking and choosing activities for the lesson?**

• **In what ways do you see this lesson being most relevant to your learners?**

• **How has the message of this passage of Scripture touched your life, and how can you share that with your students?**

Point out that in the future when they use this Lesson Planning Guide, they will write in only the activities they actually plan on using. If you have chosen to do so, give each teacher a three-ring binder in which to file lesson plan sheets. Suggest that part of each teacher's after-class evaluation process can be to make notations on the pages. These saved lesson plans can be wonderful tools for future planning. Dismiss with prayer.

Bibliography

Bolton, Barbara, Wesley Haystead, and Charles T. Smith. *Everything You Want to Know About Teaching Children*. Ventura, CA: Regal Books, 1987.

Ciona, John R. *Solving Church Education's Ten Toughest Problems*. Wheaton, IL: Victor Books, 1990.

Coleman, Robert E. *The Master Plan of Discipleship*. Old Tappan, NJ: Fleming H. Revell, 1987.

Costa, A.L. (Ed.). *Developing Minds: A Resource Book for Teaching Thinking*. Alexandria, VA: Association for Supervision and Curriculum Development, 1985.

Covey, Stephen R. *Principle-Centered Leadership*. New York: Summit Books, 1991.

Crabb, Lawrence J., Jr. *Understanding People*. Grand Rapids, MI: Zondervan, 1987.

Dobson, James, and Gary Bauer. *Children at Risk*. Waco, TX: Word, Inc., 1990.

Elkind, David. *Miseducation: Preschoolers at Risk*. New York: Alfred A. Knopf, 1987.

Fine, Eddie, and Billye Joyce. *Teachers Are Made, Not Born*. Cincinnati, OH: Standard Publishing, 1990.

Flynn, Leslie. *Nineteen Gifts of the Spirit*. Wheaton, IL: Victor Books, 1974.

Ford, LeJoy. *Design for Teaching and Training*. Nashville, TN: Broadman Press, 1978.

Friedeman, Matt. *The Master Plan of Teaching*. Wheaton, IL: Victor Books, 1990.

Gangel, Kenneth O. *Twenty-Four Ways to Improve Your Teaching*. Wheaton, IL: Victor Books, 1974.

Gangel, Kenneth O. *Unwrap Your Spiritual Gifts*. Wheaton, IL: Victor Books, 1984.

Garlett, Marti Watson. *Who Will Be My Teacher?* Waco, TX: Word, Inc., 1985.

Grant, Reg, and John Reed. *Telling Stories to Touch the Heart*. Wheaton, IL: Victor Books, 1990.

Gregory, John Milton. *The Seven Laws of Teaching*. Grand Rapids, MI: Baker Book House, 1981.

Haystead, Wes. *Everything You Want to Know About Teaching Young Children*. Ventura, CA: Regal Books, 1989.

Haystead, Wes. *Teaching Your Child About God*. Ventura, CA: Regal Books, 1981.

Hendricks, Dr. Howard. *Teaching to Change Lives*. Portland, OR: Multnomah Press, 1987.

Highet, Gilbert. *The Art of Teaching.* New York: Alfred A. Knopf, 1968.

Horne, Herman H. *The Teaching Techniques of Jesus.* Grand Rapids, MI: Kregel, 1974.

Kjos, Berit. *Your Child and the New Age.* Wheaton, IL: Victor Books, 1990.

Kuhlman, Edward. *The Master Teacher.* Old Tappan, NJ: Fleming H. Revell, 1987.

LeBar, Lois. *Education That Is Christian.* Old Tappan, NJ: Fleming H. Revell, 1958.

LeBar, Mary. *Children Can Worship.* Wheaton, IL: Victor Books, 1976.

LeFever, Marlene D. *Creative Teaching Methods.* Elgin, IL: David C. Cook, 1985.

Littauer, Florence. *Raising the Curtain on Children.* Waco, TX: Word, Inc., 1988.

Lopez, Diane D. *Teaching Children: A Curriculum Guide to What Children Need to Know at Each Level Through Grade Six.* Westchester, IL: Crossway Books.

Lowrie, Roy. *The Teacher's Heart.* Whittier, CA: The Association of Christian Schools International, 1984.

Macaulay, Susan Schaeffer. *For the Children's Sake.* Westchester, IL: Crossway Books, 1984.

Packer, James I. *Keeping in Step With Spirit.* Old Tappan, NJ: Fleming H. Revell, 1984.

Peters, Thomas J., and Robert H. Waterman, Jr. *In Search of Excellence.* New York: Harper and Row, 1982.

Plueddemann, James. *Education That Is Christian.* Wheaton, IL: Victor Books, 1989.

Richards, Lawrence O. *Children's Ministry.* Grand Rapids, MI: Zondervan Publishing House, 1983.

Shafer, Carl. *Excellence in Teaching With the Seven Laws.* Grand Rapids, MI: Baker Book House, 1985.

Schimmels, Cliff. *I Learned It First in Sunday School.* Wheaton, IL: Victor Books, 1991.

Selig, George, and Alan Arroyo. *Loving Our Differences.* Virginia Beach, VA: CBN Publishing, 1989.

Temple, Joe. *Know Your Child.* Grand Rapids, MI: Baker Book House, 1974.

Towns, Elmer. *One-Hundred-and-Fifty-Four Steps to Revitalize Your Sunday School.* Wheaton, IL: Victor Books, 1989.

Towns, Elmer. *Ten of Today's Most Innovative Churches.* Ventura, CA: Regal Books, 1990.

Wagner, C. Peter. *Your Spiritual Gifts Can Help Your Church Grow.* Ventura, CA: Regal Books, 1974.

Williams, Linda VerLee. *Teaching for the Two-Sided Mind.* New York: Simon and Schuster, Inc., 1983.

Willis, Wesley R. *Developing the Teacher in You.* Wheaton, IL: Victor Books, 1990.

Willis, Wesley R. *Make Your Teaching Count.* Wheaton, IL: Victor Books, 1985.

Wlodkowski, R.J., and J.H. Jaynes. *Eager to Learn: Helping Children Become Motivated and Love Learning.* San Francisco, CA: Jossey-Bass Publishers, 1990.

Zuck, Roy B. *The Holy Spirit in Your Teaching.* Wheaton, IL: Victor Books, 1984.

Centers

Adventures in Creative Teaching. Wheaton, IL: Victor Books, 1986.

Bible Lessons With Learning Centers. Cincinnati, OH: Standard Publishing.

Bolton, Barbara J. *How to Do Bible Learning Activities, Grades 1-6.* Ventura, CA: Gospel Light Publications, 1982.

Crisci, Elizabeth W. *What Do You Do With Joe? Problem Pupils and Tactful Teachers.* Cincinnati, OH: Standard Publishing, 1981.

Everybody Ought to Go to Learning Centers. Grand Rapids, MI: Baker Book House.

Grogg, Evelyn Leavitt. *Bible Lessons for Little People.* Cincinnati, OH: Standard Publishing, 1980.

Klein, Karen. *How to Do Bible Learning Activities, Ages 2-5.* Ventura, CA: Gospel Light Publications, 1982.

Lee, Rachel Gillespie. *Learning Centers for Better Christian Education.* Valley Forge, PA: Judson Press, 1981.

Pratt, David. *Curriculum Design and Development.* New York: Harcourt Brace Jovanovich, Inc., 1980.

Price, Max. *Understanding Today's Children.* Nashville, TN: Convention Press, 1982.

Warren, Ramona. *Preschoolers Can Do Centers.* Elgin, IL: David C. Cook, 1991.

Child Development

Ames, Louise Bates, Sidney Baker, and Frances L. Ilg. *Child Behavior.* New York: Barnes and Noble Books, a division of Harper and Row Publishers, 1981.

Ames, Louise Bates, et al. *Don't Push Your Preschooler,* revised ed. New York: Harper and Row, 1981.

Ames, Louise Bates. *Is Your Child in the Wrong Grade?* Lumberville, PA: Modem Learning Press, 1978.

Barbour, Mary A. *You Can Teach 2s and 3s.* Wheaton, IL: Victor Books, 1989.

Gangel, Elizabeth, and Elsiebeth McDaniel. *You Can Reach Families Through Babies.* Wheaton, IL: Victor Books, 1986.

Gesell, Arnold, et al. *The Child From Five to Ten,* revised ed. New York: Harper and Row, 1977.

Ilg, Frances L., et al. *School Readiness: Behavior Tests Used at the Gesell Institute.* New York: Harper and Row, 1978.

LeBar, Mary E., and Betty A. Hey. *You Can Teach 4s and 5s.* Wheaton, IL: Victor Books, 1987.

McDaniel, Elsiebeth, *You Can Teach Primaries.* Wheaton, IL: Victor Books, 1987.

Curriculum

Acorn Children's Publications, Lynchburg, VA 24514

Creative Children's Ministries, 7427 Orangethorpe, Suite I, Buena Park, CA 90621

David C. Cook, 850 North Grove Avenue, Elgin, IL 60120

Gospel Light, 2300 Knoll Drive, Ventura, CA 93003

Group Publishing, Inc., 1515 Cascade Avenue, Loveland, CO 80538

LifeWay Bible Curriculum, 1825 College Avenue, Wheaton, IL 60187

Little People's Pulpit Program, The Train Depot, 5015 Tampa West Boulevard, Tampa, FL 33014

One Way Street, Inc. Puppets, Box 2398, Littleton, CO 80161

Standard Publishing, 8121 Hamilton Avenue, Cincinnati, OH 45231

Shining Star Publications, Box 299, Carthage, IL 62321

Word and Spirit, 6633 Victoria Avenue, Ft. Worth, Texas 76181

Learning Styles

Armstrong, Thomas. *In Their Own Way.* New York, NY: St. Martin's Press, 1987.

Armstrong, Thomas. *Seven Kinds of Smart.* New York, NY: Penguin Books, 1993.

Armstrong, Thomas. *Multiple Intelligences in the Classroom.* Alexandria, VA: Association for Supervision and Curriculum Development, 1994.

Bates, Marilyn, and David Kerisey. *Please Understand Me.* Del Mar, CA: Prometheus Nemesis Book Company.

Butler, Kathleen A. *It's All in Your Mind.* Columbia, CT: The Learner's Dimension, 1988.

Capehart, Jody. *Cherishing and Challenging Your Children.* Wheaton, IL: Victor Books, 1991.

Capehart, Jody and Gordon and Becky West. *The Discipline Guide for Children's Ministry.* Loveland, CO: Group Publishing, Inc., 1997.

Capehart, Jody, and Paul Warren. *You and Your ADD Child.* Nashville, TN: Thomas Nelson Publishers, 1995.

Carbo, Marie, Rita Dunn, and Kenneth Dunn. *Teaching Students to Read Through Their Individual Learning Styles*. Reston, VA: Reston Publishing Co., Inc., 1986.

Dobson, James. *Dare to Discipline*. Wheaton, IL: Tyndale House Publishers, 1991.

Dobson, James. *The Strong-Willed Child*. Wheaton, IL: Tyndale House Publishers, 1985.

Dryden, Gordon, and Jeannette Vos. *The Learning Revolution*. Rolling Hills Estates, CA: Jalmar Press, 1994.

Dunn, Kenneth, and Rita Dunn. *Practical Approaches to Individualizing Instruction*. West Nyack, NY: Parker Publishing Co., Inc., 1972.

Dunn, Rita, and Kenneth Dunn. *Teaching Students Through Their Individual Learning Styles*. Reston, VA: Reston Publishing Co., Inc.

Dunn, Rita, Kenneth Dunn, and Donald Treffinger. *Bringing Out the Giftedness in Your Child*. New York: John Wiley and Sons, Inc., 1992.

Dunn, Rita, and Shirley Griggs. *Learning Styles: Quiet Revolution in American Secondary Schools*. Reston, VA: National Association of Secondary School Principals, 1988.

Freudenburg, Ben, with Rick Lawrence. *The Family-Friendly Church*. Loveland, CO: Group Publishing, Inc., 1998.

Fuller, Cheri. *Home Life*. Tulsa, OK: Honor Books, 1988.

Fuller, Cheri. *Unlocking Your Child's Learning Potential*. Colorado Springs, CO: Piñon Press, 1994.

Gardner, Howard. *The Unschooled Mind: How Children Think and How Schools Should Teach*. New York: Harper Collins Publishers, Inc., 1991.

Gilbert, Anne Green. *Teaching the Three Rs Through Movement Experiences*. New York: Macmillan Publishing Co., 1977.

Goleman, Daniel. *Emotional Intelligence*. New York: Bantam Books, 1995.

Gregorc, Anthony. *An Adult's Guide to Style*. Columbia, CT: Gregorc Associates, Inc., 1982.

Hannaford, Carla. *The Dominance Factor: How Knowing Your Dominant Eye, Ear, Brain, Hand and Foot Can Improve Your Learning*. Arlington, VA: Great Ocean Publishers, 1997.

Kohn, Alfie. *No Contest*. New York: Bantam Books, 1995.

Kolb, David A. *Experiential Learning*. Englewood Cliffs, NJ: Prentice-Hall, Inc., 1983.

Lawrence, Gordon. *People Types and Tiger Stripes*. Gainesville, FL: Center for Applications of Psychological Type, Inc., 1993.

LeFever, Marlene D. *Learning Styles: Reaching Everyone God Gave You to Teach*. Colorado Springs, CO: David C. Cook Publishing Co., 1995.

Leffert, Nancy, Peter L. Benson, and Jolene L. Roehlkepartain. *Starting Out Right: Developmental Assets for Children.* Minneapolis, MN: Search Institute, 1997.

Kotulak, Ronald. *Inside the Brain.* Kansas City, MO: Andrews and McMeel, 1997.

Making the Bible Easy to Teach. Loveland, CO: Group Publishing, Inc., 1998.

Martin, Grant. *The Hyperactive Child.* Wheaton, IL: Victor Books, 1992.

McCombs, Barbara L., and Jo Sue Whisler. *The Learner-Centered Classroom and School.* San Francisco, CA: Jossey-Bass Inc., 1997.

McDowell, Josh, and Bob Hostetler. *Right From Wrong.* Dallas, TX: Word, Inc., 1994.

Nash, Madeleine. "Fertile Minds." Time Magazine, Feb. 3, 1997, pp. 48-56.

Rohm, Dr. Robert. *Positive Personality Insights.* Columbus, GA: Brentwood Christian Press, 1992.

Rose, Colin, and Malcolm J. Nicholl. *Accelerated Learning for the 21st Century.* New York: Delacorte Press, 1997.

Sayers, Dorothy. Lecture: "The Lost Tools of Learning." New York: National Review, 1947.

Schindler, Claude E., Jr., with Pacheco Pyle. *Sowing for Excellence: Educating God's Way.* Whittier, CA: Association of Christian Schools International, 1987.

Schultz, Thom, and Joani Schultz. *Why Nobody Learns Much of Anything at Church–And How to Fix It.* Loveland, CO: Group Publishing, Inc., 1993.

Sousa, Dr. David A. *How the Brain Learns.* Reston, VA: National Association of Secondary School Principals, 1995.

Stevens, Suzanne H. *Classroom Successes for the LD and ADHD Child.* Winston-Salem, NC: John F. Blair, 1997.

Successful Learning Resources Guide for Educators, Parents and Families. "The Mozart Effect." [Online] Available at http://www.howtolearn.com/ndil2.html.

Sweet, Leonard. *Eleven Genetic Gateways to Spiritual Awakening.* Nashville, TN: Abingdon Press, 1998.

Swindoll, Charles R. *You and Your Child: A Biblical Guide for Nurturing Confident Children From Infancy to Independence.* Colorado Springs, CO: Focus on the Family, 1994.

Tobias, Cynthia. *Every Child Can Succeed.* Colorado Springs, CO: Focus on the Family, 1994.

Tobias, Cynthia. *The Way They Learn: How to Discover and Teach to Your Child's Strengths.* Colorado Springs, CO: Focus on the Family, 1994.

Voges, Ken, and Ron Braund. *Understanding Why Others Misunderstand You.* Chicago: Moody Press, Inc., 1994.

Warden, Michael D. *Extraordinary Results From Ordinary Teachers*. Loveland, CO: Group Publishing, Inc., 1998.

Wilson, Douglas. *Recovering the Lost Tools of Learning: An Approach to Distinctively Christian Education*. Wheaton, IL: Crossway Books, 1991.

Wilson, Douglas, Wesley Callihan, and Douglas Jones. *Classical Education and the Home School*. Moscow, ID: Canon Press, 1995.

Zacharias, Raye. *Styles and Profiles*. 1215 Whispering Lane, Southlake, Texas 76092.

Zuck, Roy B. *Teaching as Jesus Taught*. Grand Rapids, MI: Baker Books, 1995.

Learning Style Resources

Dr. Marie Carbo, "Reading Style Inventory." National Reading Styles Institute, Box 39, Syosset, NY 11791.

Rita Dunn, "Learning Styles Network and Resources." Center for Study of Learning and Teaching Styles, St. John's University, Grand Central and Utopia Parkways, Jamaica, NY 11439.

Bernice McCarthy, "The 4MAT System." EXCEL, Inc., 200 West Station Street, Barrington, IL 60010.

Music

Brentwood Music Publishing, Inc., One Maryland Farms, Suite 200, Brentwood, TN 37027.

The Donut Man, Rob Evans, 247 Bay Shore, Hendersonville, TN 37015.

For Kids Only, P.O. Box 10237, Newport Beach, CA 92658.

G.T. Halo Express (Bible Verses to Music), 1987 King Communications, P.O. Box 24472, Minneapolis, MN 55424.

Kids for Kids, Barry McGuire, 5490 E. Butler Avenue, Fresno, CA 93727.

Integrity Music, 1000 Cody Road, Mobile, AL 36695.

Maranatha, P.O. Box 1396, Costa Mesa, CA 92626.

Motions 'n Music, Scripture Press Publications, Inc., 1825 College Avenue, Wheaton, IL 60187.

Mary Rice Hopkins, P.O. Box 362, Montrose, CA 91021.

Psalty Tapes, Word, Inc., 5221 N. O'Conner Blvd., Suite 1000, Irving, TX 75039.

Salvation Songs for Children, Child Evangelism Fellowship, 2300 E. Highway M, Warrenton, MO 63383.

Sing a Song of Scripture, Lillenas Publications, Kansas City, MO 64141.

Spectra, 468 McNally Drive, Nashville, TN 37211.

Prayer

Avila, St. Theresa. *A Life of Prayer.* Portland, OR: Multnomah Press, 1972.

Bounds, E.M. *Power Through Prayer.* Grand Rapids, MI: Baker Book House, 1972.

Christenson, Evelyn. *Lord, Change Me.* Wheaton, IL: Victor Books, 1979.

Christenson, Evelyn. *What Happens When Women Pray.* Wheaton, IL: Victor Books, 1975.

Foster, Richard J. *Celebration of Discipline: The Path to Spiritual Growth* (revised ed.). San Francisco, CA: Harper and Row, 1988.

Getz, Gene A. *Praying for One Another.* Wheaton, IL: Victor Books, 1989.

Gofforth, Rosalind. *How I Know God Answers Prayers.* Chicago: Back to the Bible Publishers, Moody Press, 1983.

Marshall, Catherine. *Adventures in Prayer.* Old Tappan, NJ: Spire Books, 1975.

Mitchell, Curtis C. *Praying Jesus' Way.* Old Tappan, NJ: Fleming H. Revell, 1946.

Murray, Andrew. *With Christ in the School of Prayer.* Westwood, NJ: Fleming H. Revell, 1972.

Torrey, R.A. *How to Pray.* Chicago: Moody Press, 1989.

Reference Books

Alexander, David, and Pat Alexander, editors. *Eerdman's Handbook to the Bible.* Grand Rapids, MI: William B. Eerdmans Publishing Co., 1973.

Beers, V. Gilbert. *The Victor Handbook of Bible Knowledge.* Wheaton, IL: Victor Books, 1981.

Gangel, Kenneth O., Howard G. Hendricks, and the Dallas Theological Seminary Christian Education Faculty. *The Christian Educator's Handbook on Teaching.* Wheaton, IL: Victor Books, 1980.

Richards, Lawrence O. *The Teacher's Commentary.* Wheaton, IL: Victor Books, 1987.

Walvoord, John F., and Roy B. Zuck. *The Bible Knowledge Commentary.* Wheaton, IL: Victor Books, 1985.

Wright, Fred H. *Manners and Customs of Bible Lands.* Chicago: Moody Press, 1953.

Resources for "Doers"

Books

Bolinsky, Mike. *Affirmative Guide to Creative Bible Teaching.* P.O. Box 833, Cedar Hills, Texas 75104.

Cavalletti, Sofia. *The Religious Potential of the Child.* Ramsey, NJ: Paulist Press, 1979.

Gettman, David. *Basic Montessori Learning Activities for Under Fives.* New York: St. Martin's Press, 1987.

Montessori, Maria. *The Absorbent Mind.* New York: Delta Books, Dell Publishing Co., 1980.

Montessori, Maria. *Childhood Education.* New York: A Meridian Book, 1955.

Montessori, Maria. *The Montessori Method.* New York: Schocken Books, 1964.

Companies and Organizations

Association of Christian Schools International, P.O. Box 35097, Colorado Springs, CO 80935.

Bible in Living Sound, P.O. Box 234, Norland, WA 98358.

Caring Hands for Ministry, 12586 Post Grove Walk, St. Louis, MO 63146. 314-514-1070. Web site: www.chministries.com.

Carraway Street, Inc., Ron Solomon, 200 Frontier City, Chanhassen, MN 55317.

Child Evangelism Fellowship Press, P.O. Box 348, Warrenton, Missouri 63383.

Christian Educators' Association International, 1550 E. Elizabeth St., Pasadena, CA 91104

Comics in the Classroom: A Learning Styles Approach. Canadian Daily Newspaper Publishers Association, 890 Yonge Street, #1100, Toronto, Ontario M4W EP4.

Cornerstone Curriculum Project, 2006 Flatcreek, Richardson, TX 75080.

Creative Children's Ministries, 7427 Orangethorpe Suite I, Buena Park, CA 90621.

Creative Publications, 5005 West 110th Street, Oak Lawn, IL 60438.

Creative Teachers Publications—Task Cards for Reading, P.O. Box 41, Williston Park, NY 11596.

Judy Instructo Puzzles, Minneapolis, MN 55406. (Also available from Shining Star Publications.)

KONOS Character Curriculum, P.O. Box 1534, Richardson, TX 75083.

Learning Research Associates, Inc., P.O. Box 349, Dept. 6, Roslyn Heights, NY 11596.

Little Christian Supply (for ages 1-3), P.O. Box 1763, Blytheville, AR 72316-1763.

Betty Lukens, Felt Books and Products, P.O. Box 1007, Rohnert Park, CA 94928.

Marcy Cook Math Materials, P.O. Box 5840, Balboa Island, CA 92662.

Mortensen Math, P.O. Box 763068, Dallas, TX 75376.

National Reading Styles Institute, P.O. Box 39, Roslyn Heights, NY 11577.

NavPress Publishing Group, The Navigators, P.O. Box 6000, Colorado Springs, CO 80934.

One Way Street, Inc., P.O. Box 2398, Littleton, CO 80101.

The Perfection Form Company (Reading Beyond the Basics for primary grades and Portals to Reading for intermediate grades), 1000 North Second Avenue, Logan, IA 51546.

Play 'N Talk, 7105 Manzanita Street, Carlsbad, CA 92009.

Sing Spell Read and Write, CBN Center, Virginia Beach, VA 23463.

Sound Reading Associates, Sharon Briggs and Ginny Sorrell, 13704 Springstone Court, Clifton, VA 22024.

Sponge Activities, Idea Factory, 275 East Pleasant Valley Road, Camarillo, CA 93010.

Writing to Think and Thinking to Write, 85 Main Street, Watertown, MA 02172.

Special Needs

Dennis and Linda Dordigan (available for speaking and music), 3102 Lois Lane, Rowlett, TX 75088. (972) 412-0880.

Joni and Friends, P.O. Box 3333, Agoura Hills, CA 91301.

Pearson, Jim. *No Disabled Souls*. Cincinnati, OH: Standard Publishing, 1998.

Teacher Training

Child Evangelism Fellowship, 2300 E. Highway M, Warrenton, MO 63383-3420.

Children's Christian Ministries Association, Iris Mears, 11314 Woodley Avenue, Granada Hills, CA 91344.

Something Special for Kids, Sam and Sandy Sprott, 477 Corona Avenue, Corona, CA 91719.

Scripture Index

Jody Capehart has been involved in education for nearly thirty years. She has started four Christian schools and served as a principal for twenty years. She has also been a minister to children for eight years. She is currently the Head of Legacy Christian Academy and also serves as the national Director of Education for the Every Church a School Foundation. She is the author of ten books and is a popular keynote speaker for school, church, and women's conferences around the country. Jody's husband, Paul, is in his twenty-eighth year of playing in the Dallas Symphony Orchestra. They have three children, two grown and one at home.

Lori Niles is a contributing author to over thirty-five Christian education resource and curriculum books for children, youth, and adults. She has worked with children in church plants and mega-churches. She is currently a contributing editor for Children's Ministry Magazine (Group Publishing, Inc.) and the founder of Bright Harvest Ministries, a church consulting and equipping project. Lori and her husband, Ken, live in Portland, Oregon, with their eleven-year-old twins, Aimee and Zachary, eight-year-old Erin Elizabeth, and six-year-old Matthew.

Group Publishing, Inc.
Attention: Product Development
P.O. Box 481
Loveland, CO 80539
Fax: (970) 679-4370

Evaluation for *Touching Hearts, Changing Lives: Becoming a Treasured Teacher*

Please help Group Publishing, Inc. continue to provide innovative and useful resources for ministry. Please take a moment to fill out this evaluation and mail or fax it to us. Thanks!

● ● ●

1. As a whole, this book has been (circle one)

not very helpful   very helpful

1   2   3   4   5   6   7   8   9   10

2. The best things about this book:

3. Ways this book could be improved:

4. Things I will change because of this book:

5. Other books I'd like to see Group publish in the future:

6. Would you be interested in field-testing future Group products and giving us your feedback? If so, please fill in the information below:

Name_____

Church Name _____

Denomination _____ Church Size _____

Church Address _____

City _____ State _____ ZIP _____

Church Phone _____

E-mail _____